Go by the Ancient, Classical Way of Calais

Go by the Ancient, Classical Way of Calais

Beverley Labbett

First published in Great Britain in 2000 by
Mousehold Press
Victoria Cottage
Constitution Opening
Norwich, NR3 4BD

ISBN 1 874739 16 1

Cover picture: *Calais Pier* by J. M. W. Turner
© National Gallery

Printed in Great Britain by Watkiss Studios Ltd, Biggleswade *for Laure*

Acknowledgements

The publishers gratefully acknowledge permission to reprint
copyright material in this book from the following:

The Diary of John Evelyn, edited by E. S. de Beer (1955) by
permission of Oxford University Press.
The Note-Books and Papers of Gerald Manley Hopkins, edited
by H. House (1937) by permission of Oxford University Press on
behalf of the Society of Jesus.
The French Journals of Mrs Thrale and Dr. Johnson, edited by
M. Tyson and H. Guppy (1932) by permission of Manchester
University Press.
*John Mill's Boyhood Visit to France: Being a Journal and Notebook
written by John Stuart Mill in France 1820–21*, edited by A. J. Mill
(1960) by permission of University of Toronto Press.
The Letters of Samuel Palmer, Volume 1: 1814–1859, edited by
R. Lister (1974) by permission of Oxford University Press.
The Journals of Mary Shelley 1814–1844, Volume 1: 1814–1822,
edited by P. R. Feldman and D. Scott-Kilvert (1987) by permission
of Oxford University Press.
Thraliana: The Diary of Mrs Hester Lynch Thrale, edited by Katherine
C. Balderston (1951) by permission of Oxford University Press.

Contents

Publisher's Note   ix

1   We Sail at 3 a.m., if the Wind Holds   1

2   The Wind is Excellent – Au Revoir   17

3   Contrive to See the Favourable Side
of Things   35

4   Le Mal de Mer   45

5   Going Abroad, Anyhow, Anywhere is
Such a Lark   59

6   Many Were the Hands that Were Offered Us   69

7   Quite Well Content in Calais   85

8   So Adieu to la Belle France, and Welcome
Merry England   101

References   127

All profits from the sale of this book will be donated to the Priscilla Bacon Lodge.

The Priscilla Bacon Lodge is a specialist unit providing rehabilitation, respite, symptom control and terminal care for people who have a serious illness, but are no longer receiving curative treatment.

Publisher's Note

For a couple of years or so Bev Labbett passed what spare time he had in the library of the University of East Anglia seeking accounts of the adventurous crossing of the Channel in the late eighteenth and early nineteenth centuries. The result was a rich haul from the diaries, letters, journals and essays of those who made the Grand Tour, or whose business or pleasure took them, by sail or paddle steamer, across the 22 miles that separate Dover from Calais: two lever-arch files of extracts, in fact – some brief sentences, others several pages in length.

He had a sense of what he would do with all this material: he spoke of it as a book that would be small enough to fit into the pocket, and short enough to be read during the 90 minutes of today's cross-Channel passage. Bev liked that image of sitting up on deck, wrapped up against the sea breeze, engrossed in a book as the white cliffs receded; he made use of it in some of his commentaries on the extracts. He had a sense, too, of how he would get there for, buried amongst the pages of typed extracts in his files, is a single handwritten note to himself: 'Ruthless pruning. Make it as lean and story-like as possible.'

By the time of his final illness, when it became clear that he would not be able to work further on what he'd come to call the 'Dover–Calais project', he had pruned the material, selecting what he wanted to include, and had begun to write some of the commentaries that would accompany the extracts. In finishing his project, and bringing it to publication, we have stuck largely to his selection. We have added the present divisions of the book and endeavoured, also, to follow the style of commentary he had established. His final words to us on the project were: 'Remember, it is not a history; it is a story.'

Yet, for Bev, that was always a fine distinction: it was the story that brought history to life. Nothing excited his historical curiosity more than the contemporary document that told of a single event in a person's life, for behind that there lay an entire biography – a personal history that led up to that moment, and a future that stretched out beyond it. It was to the document, he insisted, that we must turn to find the evidence – he always called it 'the evidence' – with which we just might, perhaps, begin to understand the story of that life.

But why this particular story – or, rather, this particular set of stories? What initially sparked Bev's curiosity were the travellers' reactions to being in France and being surrounded by the unfamiliar; he was fascinated by their perceptions of the French, and, above all, by their readiness to do what he was so reluctant to do – to generalise, and to make on-the-spot judgements. Their stories of the Channel crossing, itself, at a time when the passage between Dover and Calais was so much more an unpredictable and perilous event than today, emerged from that interest in how prejudice is born.

And there was a personal dimension to it, too, for it touched upon his own story: a very English Englishman, married to a French woman, he made that Channel crossing, himself, each summer during the 29 years of his married life – more than half a lifetime.

Paddle Steamer leaving the Harbour, Dover (1856)
William Callow
©Christie's Images

We Sail at 3 a.m., if the Wind Holds

We are going to follow the advice that John William Ward gave us in July 1814: 'Go by the ancient, regular, classical way of Calais.' And we have come to Dover.

Anxious and curious eyes turn seawards. In what state the wind and the sea? How runs the tide? When might the wind prove favourable? Will there be time enough to get the carriage on board before the tide turns?

Look: there is a gentleman, standing erect, still, on the Dover shore line, and peering across the water. Perhaps he will allow us to see what he will publish in the *Quarterly Review* of July 1817.

> *It is well known to the people of Dover, Folkestone and Sandgate that, at one time, the houses of Calais, Boulogne and the neighbourhood, are visible to them above the surface of the water, while at other times, when the atmosphere is equally clear, not a vestige of them is to be seen.*

But is the French coast in sight today? When may we embark?

Public Announcement
On the 17th of July 1720, Bernard Calvert, of Andover, rode from St. George's Church in South-wark to Dover; from there passed by Barge to Calice

1

in France; and from there return'd back to St. George's Church the same day. – Setting out about 3 o'clock in the morning, and return'd at 8 o'clock in the evening, fresh and lustie. *

Not today, alas, for today is 10th October 1786: there's a southerly wind blowing directly in our teeth and Sophie von La Roche knows full well she will have to wait in Dover.

The sea is rough,and I saw it tossing some twenty fair-sized vessels at various distances away, up in the air like a ball. I spent some time watching the flow of the waves, which bring in the tide, breaking on the shore. With might and grandeur the waves roll in, chasing each other along, then broad and towering tumble on the shore, and break with a dull thud of thunder, like a waterfall now flecked with silvery spray.

But delay gives the 56-year-old German periodical editor, author of the popular 1770s novel *The Story of Fraulein von Sternheim,* and mother of five, time to reflect on her English tour:

I revisited the harbour, spent a few moments contemplating this portion of the English coast, and gazed across the water to the shores of France, for the sea extended a mighty arm between them, and divided Great Britain from the continent, with the care of a divine precaution encircling the ever-blessed

---

* Reported in *Baker's Chronicle*

isle on every side. I rejoiced at this, rejoiced at the stormy waves before me, hoping they would preserve the English national character from any harmful contamination from others, for I would rather they were influenced by their guardian angel, the sea, than by their artistic neighbour on the continent.

She returns to her inn to wait for the gale to abate, but even a favourable wind offers us no guarantee of a scheduled arrival, for we live with greater uncertainty when we travel. Scheduled arrival times are highly approximate, conditional upon the wind staying put. This can be thoroughly irritating.

Edward Gibbon, 46 years old, under five feet in height, ex-MP, who once pronounced 'I shall ever glory in the name and character of an Englishman', is *en route* with his butler and valet, Caplin, and Muff, his dog, to his beloved Lausanne, and the Academical Library to complete his seven-volume *Decline and Fall of the Roman Empire*.

The progress of his journey, he has already observed, 'must depend on the caprice of Neptune and Aeolus', but now he has become impatient with his glorious England as today, 17th September 1783, he contemplates the crossing from Dover.

We start about one o'clock, are flattered with the hope of making Calais harbour by the same tide in three and a half hours, but any delay will leave the disagreeable option of a tottering boat or a tossing night. What a cursed thing to live in an island, this step the more awkward than the whole journey.

In April 1566, while in her Dover inn, Elizabeth, Lady Hoby, 38 years old, translator and mother of three, is writing, nervously, to her brother-in-law, William Cecil, the Lord Treasurer.

Words be small recompence for your many benefits towards my husband and me, yet I must tell you how comfortable your farewell was, and how much I am bound to you for your fatherly care. We sail at 3 a.m., if the wind holds, and as it is uncertain whether we may meet again, I wish to you and my sister your heart's desire, and beseech you to make the same account of me which you do of any you may most command.

Elizabeth wants information: she is crossing to Calais, and then on to Paris, where her husband, Sir Thomas, 36, will be the Queen's Ambassador. She asks William:

Send me word whether any child born beyond sea shall inherit land in England, though I yet have no cause to demand it.

Her question is significant, or nearly so – nearly so because, come July, she will have left Paris and be back in Dover, widowed, and pregnant with her second son to be safely born and named Thomas Posthumous Hoby.

But what of these Dover inns?
'Very full and uncomfortable', Zachary Macaulay informs his wife in 1820. Years later and, as Mrs Henry Adams writes to tell her 'Dear Pater', little has changed:

> *When we got to the Pier Hotel at Dover, our souls
> sank within us, and we said, sotto voce, 'When we
> were at home we were in a better place.'*

Despite the Channel being in a boiling white rage, and the wind growing fiercer as the night wears on, she makes up her mind that 'indefinite days of waiting at Dover' would be worse than any agony on the sea.

Perhaps the Dover hotels were always so: 'The *Ship Inn* at Dover was more intolerable than ever', Harriet Granville complains to her friend, Lady Morpeth, in July 1815, and the charges extortionate, too, to judge by Poet Laureate Robert Southey, who 'slept at the "Ship", an Inn where the character of the Dover innkeepers for fleecing travellers is well supported'.

And not only the Dover innkeepers, Philip Thicknesse tells us, but the host of every inn between London and the Channel town.

> *For this reason, a man must have a very deep purse,
> or a great share of patience, to bear with temper,
> the many impositions he will meet with, upon the
> road to Dover; which begin even at Westminster
> Bridge, and pursue him rapidly all the way hither.*

And there is further good advice for the novice traveller:

> *I would earnestly caution all inexperienced travellers
> to beware of pickpockets at Dover, and at every port
> where packet boats are stationed, and not to marvel
> at the exultant charges of innkeepers. I would
> recommend to them to pay their bills as the saying*

5

is, 'like gentlemen', without exhibiting a long face
or a wry face, always bearing in mind that fleecing
is the order of the day.

Our 'renowned sporting citizen', Mr John Jorrocks, has avoided the pickpockets of Dover and, we may safely assume, has paid his bill to Mr Wright, landlord of the *Ship Inn*, 'like a gentleman'. His long face is reserved for his journal:

At the door of the Ship Hotel, the canary-coloured
coach of Mr. Wright, the landlord, with four piebald
horses, was in waiting for him to take his evening
drive, and Mrs Wright's pony phaeton, with a neat
tiger in a blue-frock coat and leathers, was also
stationed behind to convey her a few miles on the
London Road. Of course the equipages of such
important personages could not be expected to move
for a common stage-coach, consequently it pulled
up a few yards from the door ... Mrs Ramsbottom
said she never understood the meaning of the term,
'The Crown and Bill of Rights'. Many people, we doubt
not, retain a lively recollection of the 'bill of Wright's
of Dover'.

Negotiating for a vessel

Does the experienced traveller have any advice for the novice? Yes, Mrs Elizabeth Montagu does; beautiful, witty and a leading lady in the Blue Stocking circle, she arrives in Calais on 23rd June 1776, 'wafted hither by a wind very rapid and waves pretty boisterous'. A crossing of but two hours and ten minutes, during which only she and her butler have avoided seasickness because 'I sat on ye deck tho' the Waves sometimes wash'd over my head.'

Comfortable now in 'ye best apartment bespoke for me at Dessein's* where I am well lodged', she takes a warm bath to rid herself of 'ye odour of a British Herring', and has time before dinner to write to her friend, Mrs Carter:

> *If any English pass to Calais of yr acquaintance recommend Mr Fector's packets and Capt Osborne, the civilest best conductor of Ladies in a high wind for he is all attentions and honestly told me before I embark'd that there was rather too fresh a gale, but as ye passage is perfectly safe I wd not loiter at Dover.*

Edmund Burke, MP, seems to have been listening to her recommendation for there he is, hiring a vessel for the passage from Mr Fector. 'We are informed that it is much more safe than the pacquet. We are paying six Guineas for it: and are having the bank notes changed into Louis D'or's.' But has he also heeded Philip Thicknesse's explanation of the variable rates of exchange?

> *Before I leave Calais, let me remind you that an English guinea is worth more than a Louis d'or; and observe, that the first question my friend Monsieur*

---

* Monsieur Dessein – the innkeeper of the Hôtel d'Angleterre at Calais, of which Revd Cole writes: 'A fine large quadrangle, with most sumptuous apartments & elegantly furnished: & which was preferable to all, the Master of it a very civil & obliging man.'

Dessein, at the Hôtel D'Angleterre will put to you (after he has made his bow, and given you a side look, as a cock does at a barley-corn) is, Whether you have any English gold to change? because he gets by each guinea, full weight, ten Sols. By this hint you will conclude, he will not, upon your return, ask you for your French gold; but in this too you will be mistaken, for he finds an advantage in that also; he will not indeed give you guineas, but, in lieu thereof, he has always a large quantity of Birmingham Shillings to truck with you for your Louis d'ors.

Or we might heed the advice of that other seasoned traveller, Tobias Smollett, in his amusing, if somewhat acerbic, *Travels in France and Italy*, for which Sterne coined him the nickname 'Smelfungus'*.

When a man hires a packet-boat from Dover to Calais or Boulogne, let him remember that the stated price is five guineas; and let him insist upon being carried into the harbour in the ship, without paying the least regard to the representations of the master, who is generally a dirty little knave. When he tells you it is low water, or the wind is in your teeth, you may say you will stay on board till it is high water, or till the wind comes favourable. If he sees you are resolute, he will find means to bring his ship into

* 'The learned SMELFUNGUS travelled from Boulogne to Paris – from Paris to Rome – and so on – but he set out with the spleen and jaundice, and every object he pass'd by was discoloured or distorted – He wrote an account of them, but 'twas nothing but the account of his miserable feelings.'

the harbour, or at least to convince you, without a
possibility of your being deceived, that it is not in
his power.

Not that Tobias is always as resolute as he will have
us believe. Listen to him complaining, in June 1763, at
paying over the odds to be conveyed to Boulogne.

The hire of a vessel from Dover to Boulogne is
precisely the same as from Dover to Calais, five
guineas; but this skipper demanded eight, and, as I
did not know the fare, I agreed to give him six. We
embarked between six and seven in the evening and
found ourselves in the most wretched hovel, on board
what is called a Folkestone cutter. The cabin was so
small that a dog could hardly turn in it, and the
beds put me in mind of the holes described in some
catacombs, in which the bodies of the dead were
deposited, being thrust in with the feet foremost;
there was no getting into them end-ways, and indeed
they seemed so dirty, that nothing but extreme
necessity could have obliged me to use them.

Next time, perhaps, he will have the sense to pay heed
to J. W. Ward's advice, and stick to the classical route
via Calais.

But there *are* bargains to be had, as Joseph Farington,
artist and diarist, discovers. He has arrived at Dover, at
6.45 on the morning of 28th August 1802, having taken
the 'safe and expeditious London Mail Coach' that
departed from Lombard Street the previous evening. He
is accompanied by his friends, 'Mr James Moore, Surgeon,
and Mr Halls, a Student of the Royal Academy'.

Immediately on our arrival we were accosted by two or three Masters of Packets and Vessels. Having looked into two of them we preferred the larger, called the Favorite. Captain Hammond, who I believe seeing He might possibly lose us if He raised his demand higher, offered to take us for Half a guinea each person, the price proposed for the smaller vessel. He first signified that a guinea wd. be the price ... A good bargain, for now, three hours and 35 minutes from Dover, we are being placed against the Pier in the harbour of Calais.

A bargain, indeed, but sporting John Jorrocks does even better, when surrounded by all manner of touts and captains soliciting for his custom.

'Bon jour, me Lor',' said a gaunt French sailor in earrings, and a blue-and-white Jersey shirt, taking off a red night-cap with mock politeness. 'You shall be cross.' 'What's that about?' inquires Mr. Jorrocks – 'cross! what does the chap mean?' 'Ten shillin', just, me Lor',' replied the man. 'Cross for ten shillings,' muttered Mr. Jorrocks, 'vot does the Mouncheer mean? Hope he hasn't picked my pocket.' 'I – you – vill,' said the sailor slowly, using his fingers to enforce his meaning, 'take to France,' pointing south, 'for ten shillin' in my batteau, me Lor',' continued the sailor with a grin of satisfaction, as he saw Mr. Jorrocks begin to comprehend him. 'Ah! I twig – you'll take me across the water,' said our citizen, chuckling at the idea of understanding French and being called a Lord – 'for ten shillings – a half-sovereign, in fact.'

But the discussion is interrupted, first by one tout for the *Royal George* which, he claims, 'sails with a king's messenger and despatches for all foreign parts', then by another for the *Brocklebank* – 'winds made especially to suit her' – and then by the captain of a French mail-packet who 'vod take him for half less than noting'. But Mr Jorrocks is not confused by this: he beats down the price, finally arriving at a rock-bottom five shillings and, 'like a true-born Briton', promises his patronage to the *Royal George*, leaving the French captains to shrug their Gallic shoulders and wander off muttering, 'my Lor' Rosbif' and 'Monsieur God-dem'.

The sights of Dover

Your passage is secured, but, given the unpredictability of departure times, what's to do in the meantime? A stroll through the town, perhaps? Why, look: there, standing on Dover pier itself, are William and Dorothy Wordsworth.

> *From the Pier's head, musing, and with increase*
> *Of wonder, I have watched this sea-side Town,*
> *Under the white cliff's battlemented crown,*
> *Hushed to a depth of more than Sabbath peace:*
> *The streets and quays are thronged, but why disown*
> *Their natural utterance? whence this strange release*
> *From social noise – silence elsewhere unknown? –*
> *A Spirit whispered, 'Let all wonder cease;*
> *Ocean's o'erpowering murmurs have set free*
> *Thy sense from pressure of life's common din;*
> *As the dread Voice that speaks from out the sea*
> *Of God's eternal Word, the Voice of Time*

Doth deaden, shocks of tumults, shrieks of crime,
The shouts of folly, and the groans of sin.'*

Or why not the cliff? Shakespeare's Cliff is a must for the literati. What was it that Lear said atop the cliff?

Here's the place; stand still.
How fearful
And dizzy 'tis, to cast one's eyes so low!
The crows and choughs that wing the midway air
Show scarce so gross as beetles: half-way down
Hangs one that gathers samphire, dreadful trade!
Methinks he seems no bigger than his head:
The fishermen that walk upon the beach
Appear like mice: and yond tall anchoring bark,
Diminished to her cock; her cock a buoy
Almost too small for sight; the murmuring surge
That on the unnumbered idle pebbles chafes,
Cannot be heard so high: I'll look no more,
Lest my brain turn, and the deficient sight
Topple down headlong.

The painter, Benjamin Haydon, is determined to walk upon Shakespeare's Cliff. He is young still, only 22 – it will be several years before he is called to give expert witness on the merits of Lord Elgin's Marbles – but it is King Lear who fascinates him. An approaching thunderstorm in July 1808 causes him to dash to the cliff's top.

Nothing can be more awful than the rumbling echo among the heights, and the illumined sea at intervals,

---

* 'At Dover', composed 1837

*where for an instant you can see ships labouring in
surge, and now again be buried in darkness ... such
groaning of roaring wind and rain, I never remember
to have heard – The wind blows as if't will blow its
last, the rattling shower rises on the blast, the speedy
gleams the darkness swallow, loud, deep, and long
the thunder bellows – I return drenched with rain,
and exhausted with walking – I fancy Lear with his
White hair, which the impetuous blasts catch in their
fury and makes nothing of uttering imprecations on
his fiend-like daughters, and defying the lightening
to singe his white head, and am going to spend the
whole evening in reading it.*

Sir Walter Scott, returning on 9th November 1826
from Paris and the outrageously civil French – 'they drive
one half-mad with compliments' – offers a more prosaic
view, from the deck of his Dover-bound packet:

*The cliff, to which Shakespeare has given his
immortal name, is as all the world knows, a great
deal lower than his description implies. Our Dover
friends, justly jealous of the reputation of their cliff,
impute this diminution of its consequence to its
having fallen in repeatedly since the poet's time. I
confess I think it fully more likely that the
imagination of Shakespeare, writing perhaps at a
period long after he may have seen the rock, has
described it such as he conceived it to have been.*

And that, of course, is precisely the way young Haydon
conceives it to be:

*I staid on the clift of Shakespeare till twilight was
far advanced, and as I moved down, towards Town,
and turned round to take a last look for that night
the clift towered in the Sky and was almost lost in
the embruno tint of twilight, how grand it would be,
it flashed into my mind, if there [were at] the top a
Colossal Statue of Britannia, with her Lion at her
feet, surveying France with a lofty air. If this
remained alone when England becomes a desert, how
poetical would this and its White cliffs be when
lighted up by the rising or engoldened by the setting
Sun.*

Alternatively, there is always Dover Castle. William,
Mary and Dorothy Wordsworth will not be sailing till
later this morning of 11th July 1820. There is sufficient
time, then, to walk to the castle before breakfast. It is
'not rich or beautiful in its architecture,' but it 'appears
even *sublime*, from its immense height and bulk'.

*After ascending above a hundred stone steps, we
were greeted by the slender tinkling of a bell, a
delicately wild sound in that place. It is fixed at the
top of a pillar, on which is inscribed a poetical
petition on behalf of the prisoners confined above
in the Castle.*

Or, if not the castle, what about a walk along the
beach, perhaps? You'll see there the 16-year-old John
Ruskin turning his waiting to profitable use and gathering information with all manner of educational possi-
bilities. There he is, on the shingle, beneath the chalk
range of Shakespeare's Cliff, sitting, filling his notebook.

There is a bed of stiff white clay containing nodules of radiating pyrites, which are scattered over all the beach by the sea. I have found large masses of lustrous yellow pyrites (in one specimen formed upon a nodule of blue iron-stone). This mineral on the least exposure to the air is decomposed, the pyrites becomes dull, and falls into dust at a touch, and a yellow sulphureous efflorescence appears upon the fracture, not on the exterior, which is usually renaform, and coated with brown oxide of iron, which I have found likewise on the beach in large masses, and sometimes even hematitic irons, and liver pyrites.

Sophie von La Roche, meanwhile, is spending the day of 11th October 1786 shopping.

I've just bought the September and October numbers of the 'Lady's Magazine'. Maybe I should have procured them all, as they contain very nice essays, most useful for the information of my sex, as, for example, An idea of true philosophy and wisdom; On the spirit of contradiction; Educational institutes; Medical notes for women; Blind delusions of love; A fine picture of the value of a loyal stepmother ... I was informed too late of the publication of a handbook for ladies dealing with feminine interests and amusements, and directions as to how to become prosperous with honour.

But there is good news, at last. After a three-day wait, the wind has veered and Sophe von La Roche is off at midday with the French mail-boat:

Adieu, England! Be thou ever as fair as when I beheld thee, and as virtuous as I believe thou art. Windsor, Richmond, I shall never forget you more.

The Wind is Excellent – Au Revoir

Begin at the beginning

'I know your love of method, and that you will be angry with me if I do not begin at the beginning,' writes Revd Thomas Frognall Dibden, D.D., on 20th April 1818. A Member of the Royal Academy at Rouen, and of the Academy of Utrecht, Thomas is about to embark upon his picturesque tour of France and Germany. And what a joyful beginning it has proved to be.

It was surely on one of the finest of all fine days that I left my home, on the 14th of the present month, for the land of castles, churches and ancient chivalry. The wind from the south-east was blowing pretty smartly at the time; but the sky was without a cloud, and I could not but look upon the brilliancy of every external object as a favourable omen of the progress and termination of my tour.

A farewell

Picture a party of four coaches, three wagons and about 40 horses on the beach at Dover. There are the final farewells and then the horse-driven coaches enter the water, so leaving 55-year-old diarist, John Evelyn, to stand and gaze, and later write:

13th November 1675. At Dover, Mrs Godolphin delivered me her Will, which her Husband had given her leave to make, & absolutely to dispose of all her fortune, which was in value better than 4000 pounds: then after prayers the next morning my Lord having delivered me before his Letters of Attourney, Keyes, Seale, & his Will, (it being Sonday-morning and a glorious day) We took solemn leave of one another upon the Beach, the Coaches carrying them into the sea to the Boats, which delivered them to Cap: Gunmans Yacht the Mary: and so I parted with my Lord, my sonn, & the person in the world whom I esteemed as my owne life Mrs Godolphin; being under saile, the Castle gave them 17 Gunns, & Cap: Gunman answered with 11: Hence I went to Church to beg a blessing on their Voyage. The Ministers text was 1.Joh: 5.4.

Mrs Godolphin (née Margaret Blagge), 23, five months married, but is not living with her husband, yet. 'My Lord' is Baron Berkeley, 68, Ambassador to France, and recovered from a 'fit of Apoplexie thanks to the application of hotpans and spirit of amber to the head'. Captain Gunman, ex-naval captain, 'a sober, frugal, chereful and temperat man' will die in Calais (1685) 'taken away by the gangrene which happen'd in his cure upon his unhappy fall from the peere of Calais'.

As for John Evelyn, himself, he and Mrs Godolphin have their memories of a special spiritual relationship, signed on the 16th October 1672 in an 'inviolable friendship pact'. For Margaret, it has been a turbulent three years: should she marry the diplomat Sidney Godolphin or retreat into a solitary religious life?

Throughout this time Evelyn has frequently counselled her.

Now, best leave them to their privacy as they bid each other farewell and disappear their separate ways, thus leaving the beach empty for part of Matthew Arnold's poem, *Dover Beach*, capturing, maybe, something of Evelyn's mood.

The sea is calm tonight.
The tide is full, the moon lies fair
Upon the straits; – on the French coast the light
Gleams and is gone; the cliffs of England stand,
Glimering and vast, out in the tranquil bay.
Come to the window, sweet is the night air!

Only from the long line of spray
Where the sea meets the moon-blanched land,
Listen! you hear the grating roar
Of pebbles which the waves draw back, and fling,
At their return, up the high strand,
Begin, and cease, and then again begin,
With tremulous cadence slow, and bring
The eternal note of sadness in.

Another farewell

On the morning of 25th April 1816 the wind has shifted and the captain is anxious to set sail; he cannot wait any longer. Henry Hobhouse has been up since 8 o'clock but only with some considerable difficulty has he succeeded in waking his friend, Lord Byron. Eventually, Byron emerges from the *Ship Inn* and, taking Hobhouse's arm, walks through a lane of spectators down to the quay for what will prove to be his last steps on English soil. Hobhouse notes in his diary:

> *He got on board a little after nine: the bustle kept Byron in spirits, but he looked affected when the packet glided off. I ran to the end of the wooden pier, and as the vessel toss'd by as through a rough sea & contrary wind saw him again – the dear fellow pulled off his cap & wav'd it to me – I gazed until I could not distinguish him any longer – God bless him for a gallant spirit and a kind one.*

Hobhouse wants to sail with him, but – so rumour has it – has been unable to secure a passport because his recently published book is considered too favourable to Napoleon. Byron has spoken of returning in a year or so; he has also confided to Hobhouse that he feels a presentiment that, this time, his absence will be a long one. Byron's foreboding is accurate: the two will meet on the continent in a couple of months time, but Byron will never return to England.

Thomas Carlyle with time to read a letter

En route for an autumnal fortnight in Paris, Thomas Carlyle, bachelor, 28, misses the Dover–Calais ferry by one and a half minutes on 20th October 1824. This misfortune has a significant consequence: when he travels the next day it will be with a letter he found on his return to his Dover lodgings from Jane Welsh, 22, his future wife.

So, imagine Carlyle pondering that letter on the crossing in bright weather. We can see him smiling from time to time; see a frown and a concentrated re-reading of one section; then he stops, and looks out over a calm, sunny seascape, before returning to ponder the letter's ending. Finally, he folds it away.

What does it tell him? It is a private letter and should be left so, perhaps. But let's disregard Carlyle telling Jane, in his reply from the Hôtel de Wagram, Paris, one week later, that 'Your Letters, remember, are *always* for my eye alone.' Let's disregard that and be nosey.

So, go back to Carlyle, sitting on deck, smiling: 'My dear,' he reads, 'I do think I should have gone demented if your letter had not come on Monday ... I have no pleasure in life but what your letters afford me.' Then frowning. Thomas's letter of 5th October had told Jane of a 21-year-old daughter of a 'Hindoo Princess', Miss Kitty Kirkpatrick, 'not unbeautiful and sole mistress of herself and £50,000', yet 'meek and modest as a quakeress'. In the company of 'Good Kitty', and others, Thomas had found pleasure in strolling over Dover's chalk cliffs, hearing the far-sounding ocean and seeing the distant coast of France. Now he reads Jane's reply:

With such a picture of domestic felicity before your eyes, and this 'singular and very pleasing creature' to charm away the blue devils*, you can hardly fail to be as happy as the day is long. Miss Kitty Kirkpatrick – Lord, what an ugly name! 'Good Kitty!' Oh! pretty, dear, delightful Kitty! I am not a bit jealous of her – not I indeed – Hindoo Princess tho' she be! Only you may as well never let me hear you mention her name again ...

---

* Carlyle had spoken of a turbulent, depressing inner life

Carlyle first read those words the day before, after missing the ferry, and penned a wild, immediate answer that he'd later torn up. Now, he looks up across the gentle seascape and mentally composes another reply...

No Jane! ... I know you have some hundreds of faults; yet with the whole of them ten times told, thou art worth any twenty women in the world ... we were set apart by Destiny for each other; we have chosen one another; we are one, and nothing shall part us. Together we may fail to be happy; separate we can hardly fail to be miserable. Let us abide by one another, befall what may!

He turns back to the letter and is soon smiling, again. Jane chides him, 'Oh thou Goose' for suggesting she wants to be a fashionable wife. The thought horrifies her. She seeks marriage with 'one warmhearted, highminded *dearest* Friend, whose sublime Genius would shed an ennobling influence on all around him'. He folds the letter away and turns his mind to the trip about which he will later write:

Our journey ... was planned upon a very humble principle, the hope of seeing with the bodily eye alone; and on this small scale I think it succeeds as well as could be expected. France has been so betravelled and beridden and betrodden by all manner of vulgar people that any romance connected with it has entirely gone off ten years ago; the idea of studying it is for me at present out of the question.

22

It will not always be out of the question: in time Carlyle *will* study France and publish his majestically written *French Revolution – a History*. Today, 21st October 1824, the ferry ties up in the harbour and Carlyle is, for the first time, so he tells Jane on 24th October, 'in the land of fops and pastry cooks, where vanity and Sensuality have set up their chosen shrine, and everyone that falls not down to worship them is an alien and an interloper'.

Elopement

Percy Bysschle Shelley, aged 21, and the 16-year-old Mary Godwin are fleeing London with Mary's half-sister, Jane, for Dover, and on to Calais in an open boat with a crew of two. They set sail at 6 o'clock in the evening, with Mrs Godwin not far behind (Mr Godwin has not come, feeling himself incompetent to educate his daughters). Shelley describes the departure:

The evening was most beautiful. The sand slowly receded. We felt secure. There was little wind – the sails flapped in the flagging breeze. The moon rose, the night came on, & with the night a slow heavy swell and a fresher breeze which soon became so violent as to toss the boat very much ... Mary was much affected by the sea ... The wind was violent and contrary. If we could not reach Calais the sailors proposed making for Boulogne. They promised only two hours sail from shore, yet hour after hour past & we were still far distant, when the moon sunk in the red & stormy horizon, & fast-flashing lightning became pale in the breaking day. We were proceeding slowly against the wind, when suddenly a thunder squall struck the sail & the waves rushed into the boat. Even the sailors perceived that our situation was perilous; they succeeded in reefing the sail; – the wind was now changed, & we drove before a wind that came in violent gusts directly to Calais.

Jane will later record: 'As we left Dover and England's white cliffs were retiring, I said to myself, "I shall never see these more."'

The wait for news: November 1801
'10.00am. Nov 6, 1801 – *Je pars!* The wind is excellent – *au revoir*.' So writes Alexandre d'Arblay, 49, French, émigré and soldier-cum-amateur gardener, to his wife, Fanny Burney, via letter from Dover. In exile from revolutionary France, where he stood beside the Commander of the National Guards and one of America's future heroes, General Lafayette, on the Champs de Mars, swore loyalty to King Louis XVI, and was on duty at the Tuileries on the night of 20th June 1791 when the King and Marie Antoinette left Paris in disguise only to be captured and executed.

In exile, Monsieur d'Arblay gardens, and learns from his mistakes: sowing seeds at the wrong time of year; insisting that plants running to seed have not yet reached their maturity; removing weeds that are, in fact, an asparagus bed; and delighting in transplanting: roses replace jessamines, jessamines replace honeysuckles and honeysuckles replace lilacs. 'All are moved for better effect. Whether the "effect" may be general mortality – summer alone will determine,' writes his wife. But there are successes: cabbages, for example ('Oh, you have no idea how sweet they taste,' she says). But now he is gone, and Fanny, one-time Second Keeper of the Robes to Queen Charlotte, can only wait at her West Humble country house. No phone, remember. No news in a period when *The Times* speaks of 'the most heavy gales of wind ever remembered'. No news on the 7th, 8th, the 9th, 10th, 11th. And, then, a letter on the 12th, confirming his safe arrival, and joy. Fanny replies:

> *Never shall I be able to tell you the Joy of this morning – never – never! for you could only understand it by knowing all the agony of inquietude preceding it. O mon ami! – how & which way can I thank you for all the exquisite kindness & consideration of writing to me so frequently!*

Fanny d'Arblay makes the Dover crossing

The following year Fanny Burney, Madame d'Arblay, with her son, Alex, and Adrienne de Chavagnac, will make her first Channel crossing to join her French husband. 'I cross the sea tomorrow – an element I so dread – with 2 children, & not a soul that knows me, or to whom I am known!'

> *Friday 16. April 1802*
> *As we were not to sail till 12, I had hoped to have seen the Castle, and Shakespeare's Cliff, but most unfortunately it rained all the morning and we were confined to the Inn; except for the interlude of the Custom House, where, however the examination was so slight, and made with such civility that we had*

no other trouble with it than a wet walk – and a few shillings. Our passports were also examined and ratified as readily. We then went to the Port, and the sea being perfectly smooth, were lifted from the Quay to the Deck of our Vessel, with as little difficulty as could have descended from a common Chair to the ground. The rain had now ceased, and my purpose was to remain on Deck during the whole passage.

Can she possibly know, as she is lifted from the quay to the deck, that for the next ten years she will, on Napoleon's instructions, be interned in France?

A lovers' tale
On Sunday 5th September 1784 Mrs Hester Piozzi arrives in Dover. She is on her second honeymoon, setting off for 'the finest Country in the World (Italy) in Company with the most excellent man in it'.

Last night I arrived at this Place in Company with my dear Husband and faithful Maid, – having left my daughters reconciled to my Choice, (all at least except the eldest who parted with me coyly, not unkindly:) and my Friends well pleased with my leaving London I fancy, where my Stay perplexed 'em, and entangled their Duty with their Interest.

Four years earlier, in July 1780, the then Mrs Hester Lynch Thrale approached the forty-year-old Italian singer, Gabriel Piozzi, in a Brighton bookshop. He looked, she thought, amazingly like her father.

'Will you give my daughter music lessons?'

'Yes.'
Soon she notices:

His hand on the Forte Piano is so soft, so sweet, so delicate, every Tone goes to one's heart I think; and fills the Mind with Emotions one would not be without, though inconvenient enough sometimes.

In April 1781 her husband, the son of a wealthy brewer, dies. 'I have lost my Golden Millstone from my Neck, and float once more on the Current of Life like my Neighbours ...'

Widowed at 40, with five daughters, will she remarry? What of her frequent companion, Dr Samuel Johnson? Rumour says 'Yes', if the Doctor would 'discard his bush-wig, wear a clean shirt, and shave every day, give up snuff, learn to eat vermicelli, and leave off red flannel night caps'.

But now there is dear, generous, prudent, noble-minded Piozzi. Her great friend, Fanny Burney, accuses her of being in love with him. He is Roman Catholic, not of high birth, no social position, and she is in love with him. She tells him so. She would marry him. She tells him so. Her five daughters, heiresses, are horrified. So, too, Dr Johnson. The opposition is enormous.

On 27th January 1783 she gives in: there will be no marriage. But it is agonising – Piozzi leaving for Italy via Dover. He will not acceed to her requests to see him. Instead, she sends him verses:

*Come, friendly Muse! some Rhimes discover
With which to meet my Dear at Dover;
Fondly to bless my wandring Lover,*

And make him dote on dirty Dover:
Call each fair wind to waft him over,
Nor let him linger long at Dover;
But there from past fatigues recover,
And write his Love some Lines from Dover.
Too well he knows his Skill to move her
To meet him two Years hence at Dover,
When happy with her handsome Rover,
She'll bless the Day she din'd at Dover.

Her lover has left for Italy, and she is left to wait miles away and worry, and note in her diary:

Friday 9: May
Here blows a dreadful Wind, a Hurricane almost –
God protect my best beloved, my Piozzi! he was to
set out today, but that He will not; sure he will not.
Oh but the Packet might set out last night & tempt
him aboard –

> *Deh non fidarti al Mar*
> *Deh non li presta fede etc.*

as he most delightfully sings. and will he go? & is
he gone? and shall I never see him more? never
hear him more? Impossible. I will not trust myself
with such Imaginations, they will cost me my Reason
or my life.

With Piozzi gone, Mrs Thrale falls ill. Piozzi is urged to return. Nervous, he delays. No, not on these wintry roads. Too dangerous to cross the Alps. Reassured, he finally reaches Bath on 1st July 1784. 'He lodges at our

28

old House on the South Parade: his companion Mecci is a faithless treacherous Fellow – but no matter! 'Tis all over now,' Hester writes. And it is. On 23rd July 1784, they are married. 'What a noble heart has the Man to whom I was this day united.'

And they are ostracised. She has, after all, succumbed to passion. *The Morning Herald* (10th August 1784) publishes 'Lines on a Late Piozzified Marriage'.

Most writers agree, and I know it a truth,
We all love a frolic in days of our youth,
But what shall we say, when such grave ones engage
And frolic in love, in the days of old age.

But there is no turning back nor wanting to turn back. A honeymoon tour of Europe begins at Dover, on Sunday, 5th September 1784. The windless crossing takes 20 hours. From her bed in Calais, she writes:

I write from my Bed to which I am at length arrived after a passage of twenty Hours – a Thing scarce known between two Coasts of seven Leagues distance (from one another;) and in such lovely Weather, that we never lost Sight either of France or England: the truth is, we had no Wind at all; & the Flights of Shaggs & Shoals of Maycril both uncommon at this Season, made us little or no amends for the Tediousness of a Night passed on Shipboard. Seeing the Sun both rise and set was however a new Idea gained for me, who had never such an Opportunity before: it confirmed to me the Truth of that Maxim which tells us, that the human Mind must have something left to supply for itself on the Sight of all

Sublunary Objects. When my Eyes have watched the rising or setting Sun amidst a crowd of intervening Trees – my imagination painted the full View finer than I found it – and if the Sun itself cannot satisfie the cravings of Fancy, let us be sure that nothing earthly can satisfy them; and let us set our affections as directed by Scripture, on that Place where only true Joys are to be found.

A last farewell

Percy Bysssche Shelley is writing to his father-in-law, William Godwin. Theirs is a complex relationship. Two years before Shelley eloped with his daughter. There had been the famous chase to Calais. Now they are married, with two children. But Godwin remains unforgiving, and broke – his publishing ventures fallen on stony ground. Could Shelley help financially? He has helped before, so much so that there are rumours that Godwin sold Mary to Shelley for money. Now Shelley decides that enough is enough. And, to boot, one of his latest poems, *Alastor,* is receiving poor reviews: he needs to escape. So, before leaving Dover, on 3rd May 1816, he writes to Godwin:

I leave England – I know not, perhaps forever. I return, alone, to see no friend, to do no offer of friendship, to engage in nothing that can soothe the sentiments of regret almost like remorse, which under such circumstances every one feels who quits his native land. I respect you, I think well of you, better perhaps than of any other person whom England contains. You were the philosopher, who first awakened, and who still, to a very great degree, regulates my understanding. It is unfortunate for me that the part of your character which is least excellent should have been met by my conviction of what was right to do. But I have been too indignant. I have been unjust to you. Forgive me. Burn those letters which contain the records of my violence, and believe that, however what you erroneously call fame and honour separate us, I shall always feel towards you as the most affectionate of friends.

And so the Shelleys leave for Calais, with Mrs Godwin's other daughter, Claire Clairmont, already pregnant with Byron's child. Shelley will have the time, as the ferry leaves Dover, to contemplate his own situation against that of the wandering central figure of his poem, *Alastor*.

The day was fair and sunny, sea and sky
Drank its inspiring radiance, and the wind
Swept strongly from the shore, blackening the waves.
Following his eager soul, the wanderer
Leaped in the boat, he spread his cloak aloft
On the bare mast, and took his lonely seat,
And felt the boat speed o'er the tranquil sea
Like a torn cloud before the hurricane.

The Burkes bid farewell and say hello by letter
Edmund Burke, MP, 44, arrives in Dover on 11th January 1773 with his son Richard, 15, and Richard's tutor, Revd Thomas King, 27. Speculative venturing in East India stock by his family has brought financial embarrassment to Edmund, author of an *Essay on the Sublime and the Beautiful*, but he is determined his son's education shall

not suffer. How can the father help his son do something for himself in this world?

The boy deserves it. He is not idle, has a good disposition. Now is a good time to form his tongue to foreign languages. I feel almost every day of my Life, the inconvenience of wanting them. I will take him to France. This is the time for forming him in that Language, while the organs are limber.

Edmund has decided to board Richard in a French provincial town, well away from the influence of English in, say, Paris. He has chosen Blois, whose inhabitants are 'represented as speaking French with the purity of the most exclusive Parisian supper tables'. Now, *en route*, but with time to spare, having hired a private ferry from Dover ship-owner, Mr Fector, Edmund writes to his 'ever Dear Jane':

So good Night and God bless you my dearest Jane; or at least as well as you can and may you always have rest as quiet as your Conscience. Adieu all my friends. I will please God write the moment I get to Calais. Adieu, may heaven preserve you.

They sail across the Channel on 12th January. At five o'clock that evening, in Calais, Edmund writes again to his 'dearest Love'.

We have the greatest reason to bless God for all the good Circumstances of every part of our Journey. Our Captain who has been thirty years passing and repassing, never has known such a passage; nor more than one, that approached to it. We were but two hours and twenty five Minutes from the Quay of Dover to the Quay at Calais. The wind was strong, but steady, without growing more or less, or changing in the least. The Sea very high, the Effect of Winds that have been very rough and have run in the same direction for several days past. Your poor young Voyager sat on the Deck the whole time; He stood it very well for two or three Leagues; but then, we were all turned inside out; but were well in the intervals, and in good Spirits; as indeed we had reason to be ... [and the letter ends] *... The Gates are going to be shut.* * *I send this by Captain Wood. May you be as well as we are. Adieu. Adieu.*

---

*A reference to the Calais gates. J. G. Nichols in his *Chronical of Calais* (1846) informs us that Fortress Calais had four gates: the Lantern Gate; the Milk Gate; the Boulogne Gate; and the Water Gate. Official rules governed their daily opening and closing, and the Governor was required to keep the keys in his bedside coffer.

Contrive to See the Favourable
Side of Things

For what purpose are we quitting our own shores?
That is the question posed by Seth William Stevenson,
self-professed 'matter of fact man and journalist', on
the deck of the *Prince Regent* as it approaches the French
shore on the afternoon of Friday, 17th May 1816.

> *What are we leaving England to see? A country more*
> *captivating from the richness, more interesting from*
> *the variety of its scenery? Speaking from what I*
> *have already witnessed, and from much more which*
> *I am acquainted with only by description, there is*
> *no cause for sanguine expectation that the circuit*
> *of our projected excursion will present to us, in that*
> *respect, advantages, superior to those we are leaving*
> *behind: or that we shall find, on the whole, a spot*
> *more favoured by nature, more adorned and*
> *perfectioned by art – abounding more in those*
> *features which give rise to ideas of the sublime and*
> *the beautiful, or in those peculiar attractions, which*
> *the efforts of industry, and the influence of*
> *civilisation, combine in superadding to the native*
> *charms of the landscape. No, nor where 'the growth*
> *of man', where human powers, bodily and mental,*
> *keep more equal pace with the vigour that displays*

itself in the woods, and the luxuriance that shines in the fields: where the order of society is established on a firmer basis; or where a higher standard of morality regulates the sentiments and conduct. In no country (it may be safely affirmed) are the Laws so effectual in themselves, or so powerfully yet so mercifully administered, for the protection of individual interest, and the support of national freedom. With these impressions indelibly engraven on, and proudly cherished in my heart, I leave for awhile the land that gave me birth –

Blest Isle, with matchless Beauty crown'd,
And manly guards to guard the Fair. –

my object, that of comparing again, and with somewhat more matured conceptions than on former occasion, the quantum of blessings, we enjoy, with that possessed by a great and rival state.

The principles of foreign travel

John William Ward, Earl of Dudley, 35, bachelor, ex-Chair of the Commons' Committee on sinecures, might take exception to Stephenson's answer to his own question. 'Even worse than the cant of patriotism is its recant', he has advised his friend, Edward Copleston. Today, in January 1816, the Earl is *en route* to Calais and a visit to the Waterloo battlefield.

His own carriage is loaded aboard the packet at Dover. We do not know if Ward takes his own horses. We do know that the victorious Waterloo cavalry regiments have been returning to Dover – but at a cost. 'I can see upwards

36

of thirty of these unfortunate animals,' Ward reports, 'washed up against the pier at Calais.'

The packet is tossed about in a strong but favourable wind; but, even then, there is time for him to compose and rehearse to himself a few lines – lines that will later appear in letters to Copleston, Bishop of Llandaff:

You are quite right to lose no time about taking a look at the Continent. There is no such rapid and delightful way of acquring new and valuable ideas, as by travelling abroad. They flow in upon you whether you will or not ... On the whole you may reasonably promise yourself a great deal of pleasure from this expedition. The mere idea of being, for the first time, on a foreign land, – that land, too, being France, – a country about which we have been reading and thinking all our lives, – is extremely agreeable; and the impression (to judge by my own feelings) is not soon worn out.

Ward, a shy man, is given to making soliloquies, rehearsing what he will say in two voices: one gruff, one shrill, so that people remark, 'It's only Dudley talking to Ward.' Rumour has it that the habit was picked up during his time spent as a resident pupil (1803) at the University of Edinburgh. Was it there, perhaps, that he devised his principle for foreign travel – that we should bring with us a 'fair disposition to be pleased'?

William Hazlitt will assent to that. When travelling abroad, he tells us, 'we should be as seldom shocked or annoyed as possible, (it is our vanity or ignorance that is mortified much oftener than our reason!) and contrive to see the favourable side of things'.

The rule for travelling abroad is to take our common sense with us, and leave our prejudices behind us. The object of travelling is to see and learn; but such is our impatience of ignorance, or the jealousy of our self-love, that we generally set up a certain preconception beforehand (in self-defence, or as a barrier against the lessons of experience,) and are surprised at or quarrel with all that does not conform to it.

Any disinclination towards prejudice, he argues, does not come readily to the English, who 'carry out their own defects as a standard for general imitation; and think the virtues of others good for nothing'.

Thus they find fault with the gaiety of the French as impertinence, with their politeness as grimace ... The first thing an Englishman does on going abroad is to find fault with what is French, because it is not English. If he is determined to confine all excellence to his own country, he had better stay at home.

The British snob
Of whom might Hazlitt be thinking? Joseph Farington, perhaps, who professes himself 'Grateful to be an Englishman'.

I could not be insensible to that Air of independence bordering upon haughtiness which is manifested in the English Character, but is little seen among the people I had left. Wealth, and Security, and the pride of equal freedom, together habituate the mind to a *conscious feeling of self-importance that distinguishes the people of England from those of other Countries. But if this effect is produced, if there is less of what is called <u>Amiability</u>, it is amply made up by a quality of a much higher kind, which is <u>integrity</u>. That is a word which the English may apply to their character by the consent of the whole world more universally than any other nation that exists in it.*

So concludes Farington, on his return from his six-week visit to France in 1802. A trifle arrogant, we might think? Snobbish even? Mr Farington needs be careful if he is not, also, to incur William Thackeray's wrath.

That brutal, ignorant, peevish bully of an Englishman is showing himself in every city of Europe. One of the dullest creatures under heaven, he goes trampling Europe under foot, shouldering his way into galleries and cathedrals, and bustling into palaces with his buckram uniform. At church or theatre, gala or picture-gallery, his face never varies. A thousand delightful sights pass before his bloodshot eyes, and don't affect him. Countless brilliant scenes of life and manners are shown to him, but never move him ... nothing moves him, except when a very great man comes his way, and then the rigid, proud, self-confident inflexible British Snob can be as humble as a flunky and as supple as a harlequin.

But we can, surely, make an exception of Arthur Young, renowned agricultural theorist and unsuccessful agricultural practitioner, who has made a much-delayed crossing in a bye boat on 15th May 1787? It has been a 'villainous passage of fourteen hours' across the Straits of Dover, nine of which spent off Calais, rolling at anchor, but this has given him ample time to reflect upon what awaits him:

> *The streight that separates England, so fortunately for her, from all the rest of the world, must be crossed many times before a traveller ceases to be surprised at the sudden and universal change that surrounds him on landing at Calais. The scene, the people, the language, every object is new; and in those circumstances in which there is most resemblance, a discriminating eye finds little difficulty in discovering marks of distinction.*

He will be equally unlucky with his crossing two years later, and note ruefully in his diary on 5th May 1789: 'Passage to Calais: 14 hours for reflection in a vehicle that does not allow one power to reflect.' In time, however, he will become famous for his *Travels in France* that will be published in 1792, and for his appointment as Secretary to the Board of Agriculture in 1793.

The elixir of life
He who stays at home will lead a shorter life because, so Benjamin Franklin assures us, 'travelling is one way of lengthening life, at least in appearance'. It is now only a fortnight since he left London ...

> *... but the Variety of Scenes we have gone through makes it seem equal to Six Months living in one*

Place. Perhaps I have suffered a greater Change too in my own Person than I could have done in Six Years at home.

And change he does: dispatched to England in 1757 as political agent of the American colonies, the self-educated Franklin will, in time, negotiate their alliance with France and end up signing the peace treaty between Great Britain and the United States of America.

What about speaking French?

An obligation for serious travellers suggests John Latouche.

The real traveller, the patient, inquiring and serious person ... must be a linguist ... and if we ever come to live under a purely paternal government, it may suggest itself to some future Bismarck (if we are ever blessed with one) as a useful reform, and one much to the furtherance of British prestige abroad, to compel intending travellers to the Continent to pass an examination in languages before they step on board the steamboat at Folkestone or Dover. Our national prestige does unquestionably suffer from our peculiar linguistic shortcomings; and, in sober seriousness, is it not a mistake for the members of a proud nation to place themselves, as we do, at a signal disadvantage with almost every foreigner they encounter?

But, writing to his friend, Robert Levett, from Calais, at the outset of his one excursion to Paris with Mrs Piozzi,

Doctor Johnson is all too aware of his own linguistic shortcomings:

From this place we are going to Rouen, and from Rouen to Paris, where Mr. Thrale designs to stay about five or six weeks. We have a regular recommendation to the English resident, so we shall not be taken for vagabonds ... I will try to speak a little French; I tried hitherto but little, but I spoke sometimes. If I heard better, I suppose I should learn faster. I am, Sir, your humble servant, Sam Johnson.

And what shall we do when we arrive there?
Why, we'll keep a diary, of course! 'What young lady, travelling for the first time on the Continent, does not write a "Diary"?' asks Mrs Jameson on the first page of her *Diary of an Ennuyée*.

No sooner have we stept on the shores of France – no sooner are we seated in the gay salon at Dessin's than we call, like Biddy Fudge, for 'French pens and French ink,' and forth steps from its case the morocco-bound diary, regularly ruled and paged, with its patent Bramah lock and key, wherein we are to record and preserve all the striking, profound, and original observations – the classical reminiscences – the thread-bare raptures – the poetical effusions – in short, all the never-sufficiently-to-be-exhausted topics of sentiment and enthusiasm, which must necessarily suggest themselves while posting from Paris to Naples.
Verbiage, emptiness, and affectation!

Yes – but what must I do, then, with my volume in green morocco?

'Burn it!' Horace Walpole might recommend, to judge by the anxious letter he writes from Berkeley Square on the night of 19th September 1791 to the young Miss Berry, currently in Switzerland, and about to return home through France. These are, of course, discordant times.

One thing I must premise, if, which I deprecate, you should set foot in France, I beg you to burn and not bring a scrap of paper with you. Mere travelling ladies, as young as you, I know have been stopped, and rifled and detained in France to have their papers examined, and one was rudely treated, because the name of a French lady of her acquaintance was mentioned in a private letter to her, tho' in no political light.

But Mrs Thrale will have none of this. Nothing will prevent her from keeping a journal and, as for purpose, she is quitting our shores for no reason other than to seek refuge from the burden of boredom. This, at least, is what she seems to be saying as she prepares to take Dr Johnson to Paris in September 1775.

Notwithstanding the Disgust my last Journey gave me, I have lately been solicitous to undertake another. So true is Johnson's Observation that any thing is better than Vacuity. We are now going to France.

Le Mal de Mer

Hazlitt ponders on the sea

'There is,' says William Hazlitt, 'something in being near the sea, like the confines of eternity. It is a new element, a pure abstraction. The mind loves to hover on that which is endless, and forever the same.'*

He is setting out today, 1st September 1824, on his much-delayed journey through France and Italy. Originally conceived several years before, it was abandoned in favour of his divorce proceedings. Now, made possible by his second marriage, he enjoys a fine passage by steam-packet, 'with not a cloud, scarce a breath of air; a moon and then star-lit'. Time enough then, as the shores of Albion recede, to wonder at the sea itself ...

> ... that vast Leviathan, rolled round the earth, smiling in its sleep, waked into fury, fathomless, boundless, a huge world of water-drops – Whence is it, whither goes it, is it of eternity or of nothing? Strange, ponderous riddle, that we can neither penetrate nor grasp in our comprehension, ebbing and flowing like human life, and swallowing it up in thy remorseless womb, – what are thou? What is there in common between thy life and ours, who

---

*He does add that, on the day in question, 'the sea puts me in mind of Lord Byron – it is restless, glittering, dangerous, exhaustless, like his style'.

gaze at thee? Deaf, blind and old, thou seest not, hearest not, understandest not; neither do we understand, who behold and listen to thee! Great as thou art, unconscious of thy greatness, unwieldy, enormous, preposterous twin-birth of matter, rest in thy dark, unfathomed cave of mystery, mocking human pride and weakness. Still is it given to the mind of man to wonder at thee, to confess its ignorance, and to stand in awe of thy stupendous might and majesty ... but a truce on reflections.

Stormy crossings

A stormy Channel crossing can bring with it feelings of 'agreeable horror,' says Joseph Addison. His Grand Tour, designed to prepare him for the diplomatic service (in time, he will become Chief Secretary for Ireland), begins on the Dover–Calais packet in August 1699. First stop will be the town of Blois, to learn French and report on the French. "Tis not in the pow'r of Want or Slavery to make 'em miserable. There is nothing to be met with in the Country but Mirth and Poverty. Ev'ry one sings, laughs and starves.' But first the Channel crossing:

I cannot see the Heavings of this prodigious Bulk of Waters, even in a Calm, without a very pleasing Astonishment.

And astonishment leads Addison to deeper feelings which he will later lay bare in the *Spectator*:

A troubled ocean, to a man who sails upon it, is, I think, the biggest object that he can see in motion, and consequently gives his imagination one of the highest kinds of pleasure that can arise from greatness. I must confess, it is impossible for me to survey this world of fluid matter, without thinking of the hand that first poured it out, and made a proper channel for its reception. Such an object raises in my thoughts the idea of an Almighty Being, and convinces me of his existence as much as metaphysical demonstration.

A fine point-head

Joseph Addison's calm reflection on dry land contrasts with a direct appeal for mercy from the Almighty, an appeal intermingled with the urgency of saving a hat on a rough crossing from Calais in October 1718. Lady Mary Wortley Montagu, home from Constantinople and the Court of the Sultan (where her husband is His Britannic Majesty's Ambassador), speaks of a fellow passenger:

She was an English lady that I had met at Calais, who desired me to let her go over with me in my cabin. She had bought a fine point-head, which she was contriving to conceal from the custom-house officers. When the wind grew high, and our little vessel cracked, she fell very heartily to her prayers, and thought wholly of her soul. When it seemed to abate, she returned to the worldly care of her head-dress, and addressed herself to me – 'Dear madam, will you take care of this point? if it should be lost! – Ah, Lord, we shall all be lost! – Lord have mercy on my soul! – Pray, madam, take care of this head-dress.' This easy transition from her soul to her head-

*dress, and the alternate agonies that both gave her,
made it hard to determine which she thought of
greatest value.*

One must pay tribute to the sea

After a two-day delay due to unfavourable weather,
François de la Rochefaucauld, traveller, makes the crossing on 2nd January 1784, and experiences one of the
most violent sea voyages possible.

*For twelve hours we were exposed to most disagree-
able buffetings which made me extremely ill during
the whole period. Sea-sickness has an overwhelming
quality; at every moment you think you are going to
die and there is nothing that can bring you comfort.
M. de Lazowski and my brother, who accompanied
me, and also our servants were all as ill as I was.
One must indeed pay tribute to the sea – happy are
they whom she spares.*

But just whom does she spare? Not even so seasoned
a traveller as Lord Byron is spared, not even on that
final voyage he will make from England:

*As a veteran, I stomached the sea pretty well, till a
damned 'Merchant of Bruges' capsized his breakfast
close by me and made me sick by contagion.*

Nor is Leopold Mozart spared. April 14th, 1764, and
he is making 'a heavy contribution in vomiting'. And
yet, for ever conscious of the expense of his son's travels,
he manages to find some small compensation: 'at least

we have saved money which would have been spent on emetics.'

Is young Wolfgang sick, too? We don't know, although we know he is on board, but could that possibly explain his attempt, some 25 years later, to dissuade Joseph Haydn from embarking on the same Channel crossing – his first sea voyage – on New Year's Day 1791? He is 58, too old for such a venture, Wolfgang repeatedly insists, but Haydn will not hear of it: 'I am still vigorous and in good health.' On the day of his departure for London, Mozart does not leave his side; he predicts that they are probably saying their last adieu in this life.

After attending early morning Mass, Haydn goes aboard at 7.30, but, with almost no wind, they make no more than one mile in the first four hours. The ship's captain, in an evil temper, tells the passengers to expect a night at sea if the wind does not improve. Fortunately, however, it does pick up, and then blows so favourably that they cover the remaining 22 miles in the next four hours.

I remained on deck during the whole passage, so as to gaze my fill at that mighty monster, the ocean. So long as it was calm, I wasn't afraid at all, but towards the end, when the wind grew stronger and stronger, and I saw the monstrous high waves rushing at us, I became a little frightened, and a little indisposed, too. But I overcame it all and arrived safely, without (excuse me) vomiting, on shore. Most of the passengers were ill, and looked like ghosts.

Haydn tells us that he doesn't feel the effects of the journey immediately; but, then, he will need two days to recover. And before he returns to Vienna in July, Mozart will be dead.

Stinking tar-barrel

Sir Walter Scott is one who is spared, and he is happy. On 26th October 1826 he has been up since five o'clock and on board the packet by six for a fine crossing, save having to lie at anchor for several hours in the swell outside Calais harbour.

> But the tossing made no impression on my companion or me; we eat and drank like dragons the whole way and were able to manage a good supper and best part of a bottle of Chablis at the classic Dessein's who received us with much courtesy.

So, too, actor–manager, David Garrick: he has not shown even the slightest symptoms of seasickness on his journey towards Paris in May 1751:

> My wife was a little sick, but I was as hearty as the most stinking tar-barrel of them all.

So spare a thought, then, for Eva-Marie Garrick, Viennese opera-dancer. She dreads that sea-passage – a dread based on experience. In February 1746, as Eva Maria Veigel, in male disguise, she survives an appalling, gale-ridden crossing to dance at the London Haymarket Opera. There then follows artistic success, marriage and sea-sickness again, before arriving in Calais.

Sick! Sick! Sick! Sick!

Mr Lawrence Sterne, creator of the rollicky, jolliking *Tristram Shandy*, has no sea-legs, either. Now, aged 48, and in poor health, he is seeking the milder climate of Toulouse. It will not preserve him for long, however, and he will die insolvent, of pleurisy, in his Old Bond Street lodgings. But, for the moment, in January 1762, we will find him aboard the Dover–Calais ferry.

I skip'd into the boat, and in five minutes we got under sail and scudded away like the wind.

Pray captain, quoth I, as I was going down into the cabin, is a man never overtaken by Death in this passage?

Why, there is not time for a man to be sick in it, replied he – What a cursed lyar! for I am sick as a horse, quoth I, already – what a brain! – upside down! – hey dey! the cells are broke loose one into another, and the blood and the lymph, and the nervous juices, with the fix'd and volatile salts, are all jumbled into one mass – good g – –! everything turns round in it like a thousand whirlpools – I'd give a shilling to know if I shan't write the clearer for it –

Sick! Sick! Sick! Sick! –

– When shall we get to land? Captain – they have hearts like stones – O I am deadly sick! – reach me that thing, boy – 'tis the most discomfiting sickness – I wish I was at the bottom – Madam! how is it with you? Undone! undone! un – O! undone! Sir – What the first time? – No, 'tis the second, third, sixth, tenth time, Sir, – hey-dey – what a trampling overhead! – hallo! cabin boy! what's the matter –

> The wind chopp'd about! 's Death!– then I shall meet
> him full in the face.
> What luck! – 'tis chopp'd about again, master – O
> the devil chop it–
> Captain, quoth she, for heaven's sake, let us get
> ashore.

Fanny Burney is twenty hours at sea

Fanny Burney, on the midday packet out of Dover, has planned to remain on deck throughout the voyage and to arrive in time for a 3 o'clock dinner at Calais; her son, Alex, is 'delighted with the grandeur and manliness of the Idea of being at Sea', and Adrienne playful and happy. All promises fair, yet, scarcely are they beyond the harbour and into the Channel when first 'my poor Alex' is taken sick and carried below by the steward of the vessel, and then 'the contagion of his example' prevails upon Fanny, herself.

> I was compelled to take a side view of the Vessel,
> not to shock all the party by a front view of my poor
> self. Here I was stopt, and restopt, in spite of every
> effort to follow my poor Boy, a considerable time;
> and, at last, was compelled to commit myself in
> silence to the same steward, hopeless of reaching
> him by any more active means, and only by signs
> able to summon Adrienne to be of our party.

But the little girl is unaccustomed to Fanny's authority, and simply refuses to go below; she is, after all, perfectly well and enjoying herself far too much, courted by all on deck and delighted to find herself the 'play-thing of the Party'. So, picture Fanny, lying on a hammock, and suffering from a 'sickness without a moment's intermission that tore me to pieces' throughout the afternoon, unable to reach Alex who is in another cabin, and with insufficient energy to 'counterbalance the little Gipsey's delight in her amusement and her liberty' as she sings and chats with all and sundry around the deck.

> *When, at length, I heard some one say it was 3 o'clock; I was endued with sudden power to exclaim, 'I hope, then, we are in sight of Calais?' – but what was my check, when I was answered 'of Calais? You are hardly out of the Port of Dover!' & I was then told a dead calm had completely stopt our course. In this suffering state Alex and I passed the day; Adrienne was tempted to come down to us at about 5 o'clock, and, when once I could speak to her, I found voice and breath to assure her she would be drowned, inevitably, if she left us any more, & her innocent credulity then detained her; this relieved me from almost the most painful solicitude I ever experienced.*

The near-flat calm will continue through the night, with Fanny and Alex able to snatch no more than fitful moments of rest, while Adrienne will enjoy the most perfect repose till break of day. Only after 9 o'clock will they finally venture back on deck, Alex revived, but 'still pale as death from his so wretched a day & night', and Adrienne skipping 'with the smart vulgar agility of a City apprentice'. By now there is sufficient wind for the vessel to make progress, and Calais is in sight.

Dire was the tossing – deep the groans

Our anonymous traveller is with us again, reporting to readers of the *Gentleman's Magazine* that the company has set out in high spirits on a fine day with a fair and gentle breeze, and is looking forward to the prospect of dinner in Calais, appetites whetted by the sea air. But how vain are human hopes and wishes!

> On quitting the harbour of Dover, the breeze gradually freshened, the waves began to roll, the vessel to heave, and most of the passengers became sea-sick. Dire was the tossing – deep the groans. Several of them, after paying a copious tribute to Neptune, lay extended upon the deck, or in the cabin, like logs of wood, with scarcely any apparent signs of motion, and instead of exciting the sympathy or pity, furnishing only matter of amusement or ridicule to those who felt no qualms, of whom I had the good fortune to be one ... 'You will be all the better for this, Madam,' exclaimed a perty lively cockscomb to a Lady who seemed to think herself at the point of death. 'You will have a better appetite for dinner, Madam, when you land at Calais.' 'Talk not of dinner,' said she, raising her languid head, 'I shall certainly die before we get to Calais.' The mention of dinner served only to increase the squeamishness of some of the bystanders, one of whom was thrown into convulsions by the sight of a piece of fat pork, on which one of the sailors was feasting with a keen appetite.

Perhaps it is food and the rolling of the boat that forms the fatal combination. Listen to Hermannus

Kirchnerus, Civil Lawyer, Orator, Caesarean poet, and professor of Eloquence and Antiquities in the famous Universitie of Marpurg, delivering his oration 'In Praise of Travel', and quoting from the writings of Thomas Coryat of Odcombe, Somerset, telling how he arrived in Calais from Dover:

I was imbarked at Dover, about tenne of the clocke in the morning, the fourteenth of may, being Saturday and Whitsun-eve, Anno 1608, and arrived in Calais ... about five of the clocke in the afternoone, after I had varnished the exterior parts of the ship with the excrementall ebullitions of my tumultuous stomach, as desiring to satiate the gormandizing paunches of the hungry Haddocks, with that wherewith I had superfluously stuffed my selfe at land, having made my rumbling belly their capacious aumbrie.

Benjamin Franklin also seems to think eating before sailing is to invite sickness upon oneself. He is making the crossing in August 1767 with a number of passengers who have never before been at sea, many of whom have taken a hearty breakfast. No doubt they fear they might not dine again before supper-time, should the wind drop; and if they lodged last night in a Dover inn they will doubtless have paid heavily for their breakfast and feel they have a right to it. Now they will pay dearly for it, twice over.

They had scarce been out half an Hour before the Sea laid Claim to it, and they were oblig'd to deliver it up. So it seems there are Uncertainties even beyond

*those between the Cup and the Lip. If ever you go
to sea take my Advice, and live sparingly a Day or
two before hand. The Sickness, if any, will be the
lighter and sooner over.*

The cabin is the place of refuge

Abstinence for two days prior to embarcations? Is there
no other remedy? Yes. Get into a birth and shut your
eyes at once is the palliative John Stuart Mill offers us.
It is 15th May 1820 and the not yet 14-year-old prodigy,
on his first visit to France, at the invitation of Jeremy
Bentham, records in his journal:

*After having breakfasted and discharged a very high
bill, we set off for Calais in the Trafalgar packet. The
instant I set my foot on board, I began to feel a
little sick; I therefore immediately went into a birth,
lay down, and shut my eyes. I thus avoided
seasickness: though indeed I felt a little sick at
stomach during the latter part of our voyage; for
our passage was so rough that even Mr. Ensor* was
sick, which he has not been for 25 years. The rolling
of the ship was so great that at one time half the
deck was 3 feet under water.*

An early retreat to the cabin has something further
to recommend it, as Dibden, setting out for the 'land of
ancient chivalry', discovers when he judges it prudent
to put into execution the captain's advice to go below.

---

* John Stuart Mill's tutor.

Then commenced all the miseries of the voyage. The moon had begun to assert her ascendency, when, racked with torture and pain in our respective berths, a tremendous surge washed completely over the deck, sky-light, and binacle: and down came, in consequence, drenched with the briny wave, the hardiest of our crew, who, till then, had ventured to linger on deck.

Science at sea

Perhaps it is science, rather than Utilitarian philosophy, that offers the greatest good for the greatest number. Charles Dickens thinks so: 'It is impossible for any sea to affect me,' he boasts in *Household Words*, his weekly journal.

The boat may be 'lively', the waves 'chopping' ... the deck may be oblique, perpendicular, and wet; water may pour down the cabin-stairs, and the vessel may shudder in the troughs of the sea, yet shall I serenely smoke my Havannah, peacefully watch the swoop of the seagull, and observe the land growing from the distance.

And how has he acquired this enviable defiance of the rolling waves? In part, he puts it down to the French Academy of Science.

I owe it to Monsieur M. J. Curie who has explained that sea-sickness arises from the upward and down-ward movements of the diaphragm acting on the nerves of the brain in an unusual manner. I owe it

*especially to the cure he recommends: he instructs
me to draw in my breath when the vessel descends,
and to exhale it when the vessel ascends each billow
– to keep in exact time and tune with the sea and
the ship.*

Armed with this knowledge and technique, Dickens claims himself to be 'no longer one of those ignoble travellers whom seamen sagaciously warn to windward' as, once again, he approaches the port of Calais.

Going Abroad, Anyhow, Anywhere
is Such a Lark

Striking up a conversation

Given the good fortune to escape being sick, there are pleasures to be had on the voyage, not least from our fellow passengers. The anonymous traveller we saw on Dover beach is with us on the boat today, engrossed in conversation with two gentlemen, but even as he speaks his enjoyment is tinged with regret that comes from the knowledge that at Calais they will go their separate ways.

I had regretted that we were to part at Calais, probably never to meet again. Among the many delights which I find in travelling into foreign parts, my enjoyments are often damp'd by the recurrence of similar incidents, and I have to deplore the sad necessity of putting a final Adieu to men, who had attracted my admiration and esteem by their talents, their learning and their virtues. On the present occasion, everything conspired to make me wish for a more lasting and intimate acquaintance. Metaphysical acumen, strong powers of mathematical reasoning, with refined taste for every branch of polite literature, and the charm of their conversation heightened by the graces of a simple and elegant language.

But who are our fellow passengers?
Mr Hazlitt, meanwhile, perhaps weary of reflecting upon the eternal sea, appears to derive a simpler pleasure from observing the others on board with him.

> *Our fellow-passengers were pleasant and unobtrusive, an English party of the better sort: a Member of Parliament, delighted to escape from 'late hours and bad company'; an English General, proud of his bad French; a Captain in the Navy, glad to enter a French harbour peaceably; a Country Squire extending his inquiries beyond his paternal acres; the younger sons of wealthy citizens, refined through the strainers of a University-education and finishing off with foreign travel; a young Lawyer, quoting 'Peregrine Pickle',* and divided between his last circuit and projected tour. There was also a young Dutchman, looking mild through his mustachios, and a new-married couple (a French Jew and Jewess) who grew uxorious from the effects of sea-sickness, and took refuge from the qualms of the disorder in paroxysms of tenderness.*

We must only hope that none of these passengers, being 'pleasant and unobtrusive' as they are, will express any word of complaint, for that is the way J. W. Ward will form his judgement of their quality.

> *I don't like grumbling passengers, unless they can make out a very strong case of complaint; and the*

---

* The quick-witted, swashbuckling scoundrel-hero of Smollett's *The Adventures of Peregrine Pickle*, published 1751

country you have just gone through is so fine and
fruitful, the accommodations of almost every kind
so good, the capital so magnificent, and the people
so gay, ingenious, and obliging, that I am apt to
judge of a person's sensibility, good taste, and good
nature, by the degree to which he is pleased with
them. The power of enjoying the harmless and
reasonable pleasures of life is not only very essential
to a man's happiness, but an indication of several
valuable qualities both of the heart and the head
which can hardly exist without it.

Only take a carpet bag
Practical advice, now, from the widely travelled William
Thackeray. He, too, has left Dover with the time to
observe his fellow passengers: Oxford youths smoking
cigars, assuming piratical airs and, no more than an hour
later, lifeless on the deck in the agonies of seasickness;
a Scotsman, the strings of his shirt-collar sticking out
behind his back, rehearsing aloud French phrases from
his 1803 grammar book, and practising them aloud,
'serving them up in his hideous jargon. "Parly voo Fransis.
Pranny garde de mong tait."' Later, he describes their
arrival:

While the couriers, commissioners, footmen,
gentlemen, ladies' maids, Scotchman with the shirt
collar, the resuscitated Oxford youth, the family of
nine, and the whole ship's passengers are struggling,
puffing, stamping, squeezing, bawling, cursing,
tumbling over their boxes and one another's shins,
losing their keys, screaming to the commissioners,

having their treasures unfolded, their wonderful packed boxes unpacked so that it is impossible ever to squeeze the articles back into their receptacles again; while there is such a scene of Babel around me, ah! let me thank Heaven that I have but a carpet-bag. Only take a carpet bag! You can carry everything there taste or luxury demands; six shirts, a fresh suit of clothes, as many razors as would shave the beard of a regiment of Turks, and what more does a traveller require?

Time to talk together

Harriet, Countess Granville, now safe in her Calais hotel, on the evening of 2nd January 1831, after a rough three-hour crossing, is in light-hearted mood writing to her friend, Lady Carlisle.

Going abroad, anyhow, anywhere is such a lark; not more, not less, but a lark. Neither comforts nor griev-ances are as substantial as in England. I am tonight in the humour that I like being on the road so much more than being arrived in Paris.

The weather in Dover was mild as spring, the sea calm as a pond, not a breath of wind. But that didn't last and the children have suffered *le mal de mer*. Granville and Harriet, however, have good sea-legs. She reminds him that, on a previous crossing, in February 1824, all the rest had been in the cabin as sick as dogs, while they, having both breakfasted well at Dover, had been 'in high health on the deck'. Now, they are on deck again, and with time to talk, their faces freshened by the winter breeze. An eavesdropping fellow passenger might easily catch snippets of Harriet's contributions to their conversation:

I say to my intimes, 'She is trés elegante in her habits, very French' ... 'She imagines it is English de se faire announcer' ... 'Lady M. is une des plus belles tailles going. She thinks if there is a fault, she is a trifle too slight' ... 'I am happy the decision does not rest with me, as between all the pours et contres I should go distracted' ... 'His manner of making up to her is so exactly what we all like and admire that everybody was in astonishment at her insouciance. So passione, so devoted, yet so manly, si noble.'

As they approach Calais, the conversation changes. Now Harriet is talking of friends: how Lady J. was not 'en bonne odeur with the Dicks'; how Lady S. had an 'engouement for D.'; how the Duke had a 'soupçon of gout'; how 'extremely galant Freddy was about Susan, une femme charmante'; how the Duchess had 'des crampes'; and, for some reason, thoughts, too, of the recently deceased King George IV. It must have been the journey through Canterbury to catch the ferry, she tells her husband.

Do you remember? He was received everywhere with unbounded applause ... but the contre-coup was there, trés prononce, with groans and hisses.

Watching the sun rise and set

By contrast, Mrs Piozzi is virtually becalmed throughout 7th September 1784 and made to 'linger and loiter six and twenty hours from port to port'.

> *The truth is, we wanted wind exceedingly; and the flights of shaggs, and shoals of maycril, both beautiful enough, and both uncommon too at this season, made little amends for the tediousness of a night passed on ship-board.*

Yet there are compensations to be gained: seeing the sun set and rise upon an unobstructed horizon is a new experience for Mrs Piozzi, which confirms for her the truth of that maxim which says 'the human mind must have something left to supply for itself on the sight of all subliminary objects'.

Relaxed observation

Gerald Manley Hopkins, Catholic priest, lover of colours, would understand that maxim. On deck and heading for home on 1st August 1868, he has time to think of the scenes from his walking holiday in the Alps: the egg-blue lake, the dead purple skies, the pinkish snow, the cindery lily-white stones, the butter-bright lustre, the brassy clouds changing their colour to bright red over the sundowns and to fruit-tree blossom opposite, the blue-green lakes, the grass-green heights, and the waterfall like milk chasing round blocks of coal or like the skin of a white snake chequered with black. And time, also, to observe the Channel:

Day bright. Sea calm, with little walking wavelets edged with fine eyebrow crispings, and later nothing but a netting or chain-work on the surface, and even that went, so that the smoothness was marbly and perfect and, between the just-corded near sides of the waves rising like fishes' backs and breaking with darker blue the pale blue of the general field, in the very sleek hollows came out golden crumbs of reflections from the chalk cliffs. – Peach-coloured sundown and above some simple gilded messes of cloud, which later became finer, smaller, and scattering all away.

Nothing can be more delightful than Calais

Of course, there is the sheer pleasure of anticipation. Four years on from their elopement, Percy and Mary Shelley, now with their children William and Clara, and Claire Clairmont (as Jane Godwin is now known) and her daughter, Allegra, are again *en route* for Calais. Their travels will take them to Dijon, Lyons, Turin, and then beyond – to Milan and Como. The trip will allow Allegra, born 12th January 1817, in Bath, to see her father, Lord Byron. Claire's diary entry reads:

Thursday March 12th 1818.
Walk upon the Beach. (Bathe my Darling). Discussion whether we shall go. We do go in the Lady Castlereagh with Major and Mrs Hare & some other ladies. The brine is very stormy. The Waves Mountains high. But the Wind was favorable & blew us in two hours & fourty minutes into Calais. Mrs Hare was much frightened & repeated the Lord's Prayer in her

Distress, every now & then requesting her Servant to go on with it as she was prevented by Sickness. Nothing can be more delightful than Calais. The people are so agreeable & the town so airy & agreeable.

The encounters with Byron will prove turbulent. In March 1821, Claire and Allegra will be placed in an Italian convent, and in April of the following year Allegra will die of typhoid fever.

Revd Cole reads about the Dover–Calais crossing
Revd Cole sails on 17th October 1765, bound for Paris. Firstly, however, he will pass some days in the College of Louis le Grand at St Omer, formerly belonging to the English Jesuits, but, since the Order's banishment from France, bestowed upon the 'English Secular Priests, for the Education of Youth of our Nation in the Roman Catholic Religion'. He is, he confides to his journal, perhaps the 'first Clergyman of the Church of England who ever laid in that College'.

Very fine Day. At 10 o'Clock in the Morning, I went aboard the Pacquet Boat, & arrived at Calais in 3 Hours & 4 or 5 Minutes, during which Time every Passenger was sick except myself, it being a rough Sea, tho' an exceeding fine Day: so that I sat upon Deck without my great Coat all the Passage. We had about 20 Passengers, English, French and Germans.

We have no evidence to suggest that Revd Cole, the sole healthy passenger, is spending his time reading to avoid the groans and grunts of his fellow passengers; we do know, however, that he is an educated man and that he can speak French. So, let us take a little liberty and imagine that Cole has taken with him as reading matter Abbé Prévost's *Mémoires d'un Homme de Qualité*, and, not surprisingly, he comes across an account of the Dover–Calais crossing.

Picture him, then, on that bright, sunlit morning, engrossed in his book.

In an instant, we were some way distant from the shore. But our eyes were still glued to it. Turning to my companion, the Marquis, I said, 'Happy isle. Happy inhabitants. What do they lack that could make life more agreeable? The summer warmth is not excessive, nor the winter cold immoderate ... and are they not happy in the moral order? They know how to preserve their liberty against the attacks of tyrants. Their laws are wise, and easily comprehensible. You will not find one that does not promote the public good. Each person knows the extent of his rights. In towns and villages one sees hospitals for the sick, retirement homes for the poor provided by charity, asyles for the aged of both sexes, schools for the instruction of children ... 'enfin mille monumens de piete et de zele pour la religion et la patrie.' Which man of good sense would not prefer these wise and religious foundations to our convents and our monasteries, where one knows only too well that they sloth and bedeck themselves in the name of a worldly disdain and the contemplation of celestial truths?'

At this point his travelling companion interrupted his effusion of esteem for the English. 'Sounds to me as if you have become a Protestant.'

'No,' he replied, 'I am in the case of religion what I believe I must be; it is neither the world of catholicism nor protestantism that determines my position. It is the knowledge of the truth that I believe I acquired a long time ago through God's favour and my reflexions.'

And so the talk between the two went on and on, for so long ... instead of the coast of England, now lost from view, we began to see the French coast, and the wind continued to be favourable and we arrived 'en fort peu de tems' in the port of Calais.

And so, too, does Revd Cole.

Many Were the Hands that
Were Offered Us

Spying the French coast

The sighting of the destination is a significant moment
– the haven. Our anonymous traveller in 1815 takes up
his story.

> *After upwards of three hours, we came in full view
> of the coast of France, at which I gazed with
> considerable interest, although the prospects had
> nothing particular to recommend them, either in
> respect of grandeur or beauty. What then was it which
> rendered them so interesting? I answer: Novelty,
> which never fails to give an interest to objects which
> have nothing else to recommend them, and is a
> principal source of the pleasures which we derive
> from foreign travel ... and this pleasure I felt in a
> considerable degree on the first view of the French
> coast and the town of Calais.*

Approaching Calais: look out for the church tower

Look out for the tower as you approach Calais, and
imagine John Ruskin doing the same in early May 1856.
It is, he says, 'the epitome of all that makes the Continent
of Europe interesting ... and completely expresses that
agedness in the midst of active life which binds the new

and the old into harmony'. Novelty is not the attraction for him, a seasoned continental traveller, but later, on land and with time to inspect, Ruskin will begin the fourth volume of *Modern Painters* with his eulogy on the tower, his 'glorious thing' as Rossetti will call it.

I cannot find words to express the intense pleasure I have always in finding myself, after a prolonged stay in England, at the foot of the old tower of Calais church. The large neglect, the noble unsightliness of it; the record of its years written so visibly, yet without any sign of weakness or decay; its stern wasteness and gloom, eaten away by the Channel winds, and overgrown with the bitter sea grasses; its slates and tiles all shaken and rent, and yet not falling; its desert of brickwork full of bolts, and holes and ugly fissures, and yet strong like a bare brown rock; its carelessness of what any one thinks or feels about it, putting forth no claim, having no beauty or desirableness, pride nor grace; yet neither asking for pity; not, as ruins are, useless and piteous, feebly or fondly garrulous of better days; but useful still, going through its daily work – as some old fisherman beaten grey by storm, yet drawing his daily nets; so it stands, with no complaint about its past youth, in blanched and meagre massiveness and servicableness, gathering human souls together underneath it; the sound of its bells for prayer still rolling through its rents; and the grey peak of it seen far across the sea, principal of the three that rise above the waste of surfy sand and hillocked shore – the lighthouse for life, and the belfry for labour, and this for patience and praise.

Mrs Thrale's surprise

After six hours at sea, Mrs Thrale steps ashore at Calais on 17th September 1775 with her husband, and her children, including 11-year-old daughter, Queeney ('whose sickness oppressed her beyond conception') and Dr Samuel Johnson. They are bound for Paris – not Italy, of which Johnson has told his friend, Boswell, 'A man who has not been in Italy, is always conscious of an inferiority, from his not having seen what it is expected a man should see. The grand object of travelling is to see the shores of the Mediterranean.'

Never mind: Calais and Paris will have to do, and at Calais Mrs Thrale is surprised.

I was vastly surprized when I landed at Calais to see the Soldiers with Whiskers and the Women mostly so ugly and deform'd. They however seemed desirous to hide their frightfulness, for all wore long Clokes of Camlet that came down to their Heels.

Getting ashore

The calm which has caused Fanny Burney's frightfully slow passage to Calais, in April 1802, has, at least, had the advantage of allowing their packet to tie up so close and even with the quay that she requires no help to step from the deck on to land.

Many, however, were the hands that were offered us; the quay was lined with crowds of people, men, women, Children, & certain amphibious females, who might have passed for either sex or any thing else in the world, except what they really were, European

71

Women! Their Man's Hats, man's Jackets, & man's shoes, their burnt skins & most savage looking peticoats, hardly reaching, nay, not reaching their knees, would have made me instantly believe any account I could have heard of their being just imported from the wilds of America.

By contrast, Lord Malmesbury is prevented from landing on 23rd February 1832. The weather was fine at the outset, but fog has descended and, with it, a hard, black frost. And, to make matters worse, Captain Bushill, neglecting to sound for depth, has run aground, five miles west of Calais.

We were within a stone's throw of the shore, but not allowed to land on account of quarantine for cholera. Cold intense, twenty degrees, and no possibility of a fire. The Coastguard watched us all night to prevent our landing, as the vessel was high and dry at low water, and also to assist in case of danger.

The following day, on a rising tide, they are able to enter Calais harbour.

We were inspected by Commission sanitaire. On asking a member of how soon we were to be released, he replied 'Melez-vous de vos affaires. Ven I come I come.'

Sea-nymphs and mermen
But does a low-tide arrival at Calais inevitably mean a wait for the next high tide? It seems not, for there is the

landscape and marine painter, William Callow, eagerly returning to Paris to resume his studies, interrupted by the riots of the previous year. In a few years time, the Society of Water-Colour Artists will elect him a member in recognition of his 'dashing style of execution' learned from the French School. But today, 2nd February 1831, his ferry is unable to enter Calais harbour and he is amongst the passengers transferred to small boats and, waiting for them in the shallows, are the women porters who will carry them to dry land.

How well I remember the woman who carried me, saying 'Tenez ferme,' and bidding me clasp her tightly round the neck.

Some passengers, however, reports Thomas Manning, son of a Norfolk Rector, to his friend, Charles Lamb, do not seem to understand that they have to 'throw themselves into the arms of these sea-nymphs'. They remain sitting in the stern of the boat being deluged with sea-spray as they are rowed ashore, their ferry having just run aground in the midst of the breakers.

Fortunately I have already myself on the backs of two of them without reserve. They are bearing me dryly on shore. Alas one poor gentleman has slipped through their fingers and fallen over head and ears into the sea.

Interned, on Napoleon's order, Manning, himself, will eventually slip through French fingers by obtaining a passport for China. He will be the first European ever to reach Lhassa.

Mrs Elizabeth Montagu and her companion, Mrs Carter, are also being carried ashore, but not by any 'sea-nymphs'. The beautiful and witty conversationalist (much admired by Dr Johnson), and a leading lady among the circle of Blue Stockings, seems to have taken little pleasure in the experience, to judge from the letter she'll later write from Spa to Mrs Vesey:

> *Spa ye 14 of July, 1763.*
> *At Calais on the shore we were met by certain mermen crown'd with sea weeds, who carried Mesdames Carter and Montagu on their backs; as the petticoats were a little discomposed in this way of walking on other mens legs, it is better not to be too minute in the description of it; all I shall say, is that Phoebus who has a penetrating eye, told his nine prudes of Mrs Carter's want of decorum, and advised them not to be so intimate with her for future. They redden'd, pull'd up their heads, and mutter'd something about Daphne, which you may imagine the God of Witt and parent of repartee answer'd very smartly.*

Travellers will be accosted

On both sides of the water Benjamin Franklin suffers from the impositions of assorted boatmen and porters, to the extent that he cannot decide which are the more rapacious, the English or French, although 'the latter have, with their Knavery, the most Politeness'. But Fanny Burney takes a kindlier view. Her vessel, now docked beside the Calais quay, is swiftly and silently filled with men who, 'though dirty and mean, were so civil and gentle that they could not displease'.

When we were quitting it, however, this tranquility was abruptly disappeared; for in an instant they rushed round me, one demanding to carry Alex, another, Adrienne, another seizing my Ecritoire, another my arm – & some one, I fear, my Parasol, since I have never been able to find it since. However, not to be scandalous, I am by no means sure it was not left at the Inn.

Our agriculturalist, Arthur Young, also finds himself assailed on the Calais quay, by 'waiters from the various hotels, recommending their various houses with clamorous din'.

They were all eager to lay hold of the skirt of an Englishman – and happy was the man who had the address to march off in triumph with an English guest.

Having been shown the spot where Louis XVIII landed on his restoration the previous year, the shape and measure of his foot being precisely marked upon the pavement, he hears a voice in the crowd: 'Oui, Monsieur, par ici pour l'Hotel Dessein.' Assured that it is the very hotel that figures so prominently in Sterne's *Sentimental Journey*, he asks to be conducted there, and 'I had the good fortune to find very comfortable accommodations there.'*

---

* Rumour has it, so Thicknesse tells us, that Monsieur Dessein has become one of the richest men in Calais: 'By uniting the profitable business of a banker to that of a publican; by studying the *Gout* of the English nation, and changing their gold into French currency, he has made, they say, a *Demi-Plum.'*

Other ways of getting ashore: walking along the sands
Lady Coke leaves Dover in the early hours of 20th June 1764. By 8.30 a.m. she is within two leagues of Calais, but then the wind backs, to become directly contrary and the captain casts anchor. 'I suggest you go ashore in that little boat [otherwise] you'll have to wait till 5.00pm this evening when the tide turns.'

This determined me to follow the advice, but the waves, which have no respect for a little Boat, made me so rough a visit, that I was as much wet as if I had been dip'd in the sea, & a circumstance that made it still more unlucky – they were obliged to land me between four & five miles from Calais, & I was forced to walk all that way over very uneven Sands cover'd with pebbles, that cut so many holes in my shoes & stockings that my poor feet suffer'd very much, & notwithstanding my courage (of which you Know I have a good deal) I was obliged to sit down twice on the sands not able to bear the pain. During this time, two french Officers came by on Horse back & offer'd to get off their Horses & walk if I wou'd accept of one of them to ride to the town, but, not accustom'd to ride in the Foreign way, I thought I shou'd hardly be able to keep on seting sideways on a Mans sadle upon a managed Horse, so I returned them many thanks but refused the offer & with much pain and difficulty I arrived at Calais.

But there are consolations for Lady Coke, 38, and widowed. In Brussels she will meet 'the most agreeable woman I ever knew' – a lace-making, cat-owning nun, and a wonderful conversationalist. Regular visits will follow in the years to come. 'My nun is still alive,' she writes on 5th October 1770. 'Shall go and visit my nun if she is still alive' she decides in July 1773. And she is.

Or driving upon the sands

Percy Bysschel Shelley, eloping with the sixteen-year-old Mary Godwin, and Mary's half-sister, Jane, have sailed through a stormy night in an open boat, with Mrs Godwin in pursuit. Now, as the sun is rising, they have driven upon the Calais sands.

> *The morning [29th July 1814] broke, the lightning died away, the violence of the wind abated. We arrived at Calais, whilst Mary still slept. We drove upon the sands. Suddenly the broad sun rose over France. I said, 'Mary, look; the sun rises over France.' We walked over the sands to the Inn.*

In the evening Captain Davison will come to their hotel and tell them that a fat lady has arrived, who is accusing Shelley of running away with her daughter. It is Mrs Godwin.

'Jane come home,' she pleads.

'Shall I go home?'

'Consider it for half an hour,' is Shelley's advice.

The next day the three leave for Paris, and on then to Switzerland, while Mrs Godwin returns to Dover. From this moment Jane now begins to call herself Claire Clairmont – these are heady days. In 1826 Mary Shelley recalls the exhilaration, and its disappearance:

But in those early days of migration, in the summer of 1814, every inconvenience was hailed as a new chapter in the romance of our travels; the worst annoyance of all, the Custom-house, was amusing as a novelty; we saw with extasy the strange costume of the French women, read with delight our own descriptions in the passport, looked with curiosity on every plat, fancying that the fried-leaves of artichokes were frogs; we saw shepherds in opera-hats, and post-boys in jack-boots; and heard little girls and boys speak French: it was acting a novel, being an incarnate romance. But these days are now vanished: frequent landings at Calais have deprived it of its captivating novelty.

Passports are required

Or, rather, passports are *usually* required. Miss Berry, her travelling companions having forgotten to furnish themselves with such essential requirements, is prevented from landing. But she will not be delayed long.

Being well known there, they allowed them to pass, and we were just three hours from one inn to the other.

And at dinner they are visited by the Governor …

…the poor old Comte de Celie, who was for so long in England. I do not know whether this little old man considers it a duty to give a welcome to all the English who arrive; if so, he must have enough to do.

It is, indeed, his duty, and should he have enough to do, or be otherwise physically impeded, he has his deputy, as Thomas Croyat discovers when he arrives in Calais in 1608.

Presently after my arrival, I was brought with the rest of my company to the Deputy Governor of the towne, whose name was Monsieur de la Genet: the principall Governor's name (whom we saw not) was Monsieur de Vic, who hath one wooden leg. The Deputy was a very worthy and gallant Gentleman, and shewed himselfe very affable to us. For he asked us many questions, as about our King, and the newes of Ireland, &c. and very courteously intreated us; and after this familiar parle dismissed us to our lodgings.

Unlike Miss Berry, William Hazlitt is delayed by the matter of passports, albeit but briefly. He is not so well-connected and his attempts to reach the head of the passport queue are thwarted by those 'persons in a certain class of life [who] are so full of their own business and importance, that they imagine every one else must be aware of it'.

In advancing up the steps to give the officers our passport, I was prevented by a young man and woman, who said they were before me, and on making a second attempt, an elderly gentleman and lady set up the same claim, because they were behind me. It seemed that a servant was waiting with passports for four.

Age de 52 ans, cheveux brun

Zachary Macaulay is impressed at the passport office where he is obliged to wait while a sharp-looking fellow eyes him keenly from head to foot before composing his passport description. Macaulay recounts this in a letter to his wife on 11th September 1820:

His description of me is as follows: 'Age de 52 ans, taille d'un mètre 70 centimètres. Cheveux brun, front haut, sourcils bruns, yeux gris bruns, nez moyen, bouche moyenne, barbe brun, menton rond, visage ovale, teinte ordinaire.' I really do not believe that if you had been put to it, though you have known me for twenty-four years, you could have given so accurate a description of me as this Commis du Bureau des Passeports did in a few minutes.

Would Mrs Macaulay, after 24 years, really not be capable of improving upon that description of her husband? We cannot know, but we do know that the question of translation can make for all manner of *Jaunts and Jollities* as Mr Jorrocks finds out.

Early next morning, Mr Jorrocks and the Yorkshireman, accompanied by the commissionnaire of the Hotel d'Orleans, repaired to the upper town for the purposes of obtaining passports ... 'What is the French for fox-'unter,' said he, after a thoughtful pause, turning to his dictionary. There was no such word. 'Sportsman, then? Aye. Chasseur! How would that read? "John Jorrocks, Esq., Chasseur" — not bad, I think,' said he. 'That will do,' replied the Yorkshireman, 'but you must sink the Esquire now, and tack "Monsieur" before your name, and a very pretty, euphonious sound "Monsieur Jorrocks" will have.'

The officers are very queer fellows
The custom officers can be as unpredictable as the weather, as Lady Coke discovers when she arrives at Calais on 5th September 1771 after a favourable passage of three and a half hours.

The Custom House officers were so rigid that they unpacked every trunk, took out every single thing, & as luckily there was nothing they cou'd take, they made me pay the duty for two pounds of tea & six teaspoons, that I carried with me: I used to be better treated at Calais, but I owed this severity to a new Custom House Officer, who to be sure was not too polite.

Fanny Burney has neglected to enquire when the formality of the Customs will take place, and now a Commissary arrives at her hotel, demanding to know if she is in possession of anything contraband to the Laws of the Republic. She answers evasively (with 'all my new petticoats jumping in the Mouth of my conscience') that she has 'brought nothing for sale'.

'Mais, Madame – avez vous quelques Chose de neuf?' – 'Oui, Monsieur.' – 'Quelque Jupons?' – 'Beaucoup, Monsieur.' 'Quelque bas de Coton?' – 'Plusiers, Monsieur.' 'Eh bien, Madame – tout ca sera saisi!' – 'Mon Dieu, Monsieur! quand ce n'est pas de tout

pour Vendre! seulement pour porter?' – 'C'est egal,
Madame. tout ca sera saisi.' – 'Eh – mon dieu, que
faut-il donc faire?' 'Il faut, Madame – payer
genereusement; &, si vous etes bien sur qu'il n'y est
rien a vendre alors – peut-etre -' I entreated him to
take charge himself as to what was right, &
GENEROUS, – & he undertook to go through the
ceremony for me, without my appearing. I was so
much frightened, & so happy not to be called upon
personally, that I thought myself very cheaply off in
his after demand, of a Guinea & a half.

Cheap indeed, although later she will find herself having
to pay a further two and a half guineas for her additional
luggage.

Samuel Palmer, and his wife Hannah, newly married
in the Marylebone Registrar's Office (at the insistence of
Hannah's parents), have rather better luck – they will
pay nothing.

After a comfortable crossing on 5th October 1837,
followed by a rest in their hotel and a basin of nice
mutton broth, they have gone down to the Customs
House. All is well, and Hannah writes a hurried, but
cheery note to 'dear Papa and Mamma'.

We have safely arrived in France after a beautiful
still voyage ... We went into the Custom house to
see our things examined; the officers are very queer
fellows, but they pack up every thing they look over.

And Samuel adds a line, on the same page 'because at
the post office they otherwise charge for a double letter'
(finance is always going to be a problem for him).

My dear Mr and Mrs Linnell.
*I think Anny has got through this, the worst part of
her journey remarkably well, indeed very much better
than could have been at all expected ... We have
arranged so that she will have as much rest and as
little fatigue as possible and as she has managed
the worst part, the voyage, so well there can be no
doubt of her getting through what remains – with
tolerable management.*

Is the note intended to ease the Linnell's misgivings
at their daughter's marriage to this staunch churchman,
and the expensive, two-year Italian honeymoon they are
now embarked upon? We do not know. We do know,
however, that the Italian light will have a profound effect
upon Palmer's painting: muted and subtle English
landscapes will give way to indigo skies and a more
brilliant palette. 'Much as I love England,' he will declare,
'I think every landscape painter should see Italy. It
enlarges his idea of creation and he sees at least the sun
and air fresh as from the head of their maker.'

Quite Well Content in Calais

John Barber Scott is excited soon after his arrival in Calais on 9th May 1814.

So cut off from France have Englishmen been, from the time of my birth to that of my landing in France, that this event is producing a singular lightness of spirits and gaiety, and an excess of attention and curiosity. Everything around me is so new, such a contrast is exhibited in costume, manners and customs ... Thus did I write on the day on which I first landed in France, and richly did my Tour afford to me every advantage which I had anticipated.

One advantage which he does not anticipate on that day will be a 22-minute 'interview and personal conversation with *the* great man of the Age, with Napoleon himself, under the most favourable circumstances'. This will be the high point of Scott's tour, despite the ambiguity of feeling it will engender in him later, in his hotel.

We were so delighted with the reception he gave us that I must confess that we drank 'Napoleon' unanimously, in a bumper, on our return – a part of the afternoon of which, on reflection, I feel rather ashamed.

First sights of Calais

Fanny Burney's first walk through the streets of Calais allays her many 'great, though nameless fears'.

The Day was fine, the street was clean, two or three people, who passed us, made way for the Children, as they skipt out of my hands, & I saw such an unexpected appearance of quiet order & civility, that, almost without knowing it, we strolled from the Gate, & presently found ourselves in the Market place, which was compleatly full of Sellers & Buyers, & Booths, looking like a large English Fair.

The children, Alex and Adrienne, are delighted and Fanny amused at the sight of 'queer gawdy jackets, always of a different colour from the petticoats and the gold earrings worn by all'.

Even the maids who were scrubbing or sweeping; ragged wretches who were carrying burthens on their heads or shoulders; old women selling fruit or other eatables; Gipsey-looking Creatures with Children tied to their backs, – all wore these long, broad, large, shining Gold Earings! Beggars, however, we saw not – no, not one, all the time we stayed, or sauntered; &, with respect to civility & gentleness, the poorest & most ordinary persons we met, or passed, might be compared with the best dressed & best looking walkers in the streets of our metropolis, & still to the disadvantage of the latter. I cannot say how much this surprised me, as I had conceived an horrific idea of the populace of this Country, imagining them all transformed into bloody monsters.

She is astonished and pleased, too, to notice the 'innumerable pretty women and lovely children, almost all of them extremely fair'. Astonished because she has been 'taught to expect nothing but mahoghany complexions & hideous features, instantly on crossing the Strait of Dover!'

Back at the hotel she mentions this, only to be informed by the Highlander in her party of travellers that 'Calais was in the hands of the English so many years, that the English race there is not yet extinct!'

Does our Highlander, perhaps, know of the arrogant boast the English once placed above the main gate: 'Then shall the Frenchman Calais win; when iron and lead like cork shall swim'? Or has he simply been listening to that Lowlander, Sir Walter Scott, declaiming on the loss of Calais?

Lost as all know by the bloody papist bitch (one must be vernacular when on French ground) Queen Mary of red hot memory. I would rather she had burnd a score more of Bishops. If she had kept it her sister Bess would sooner have parted with her virginity – Charles I had no temptation to part with it – it might indeed have been shufled out of our hands during the civil wars but Noll would have as soon let Monsr. draw one of his grinders – then Charles II would hardly have dared to sell such an old possession as he did Dunkirk and after that the French had little chance till the Revolution. Even then I think we could have held a place that could be supplied from our own element, the sea. Cui bono? – None I think but to plague the roges.

William Hazlitt's first impressions are every bit as complimentary as Fanny's, and we know he's not always easy to please.

> *What I like in their expression (so far) is not the vivacity, but the goodness, the simplicity, the thoughtful resignation. The French are full of gesticulation when they speak; they have at other times an equal appearance of repose and content. You see the figure of a girl sitting in the sun, so still that her dress seems like streaks of red and black chalk against the wall; a soldier reading; a group of old women (with skins as tough, yellow, and wrinkled as those of a tortoise) chatting in a corner and laughing till their sides are ready to split; or a string of children tugging a fishing boat out of the harbour as evening goes down, and making the air ring with their songs and shouts of merriment (a sight to make Mr Malthus shudder!). The air is a cordial to them, and they drink drums of sunshine.*

John Ruskin draws Calais pier

John Ruskin, aged fourteen, crosses to Calais in 1833 with his parents: they have provided him with little by way of formal education but rich opportunities for travel – Calais, Cologne, up the Rhine, the Alps, Italy. For his thirteenth birthday, Ruskin received a book, Rogers' *Italy* with Turner's vignettes, which he will imitate – there is nothing better. In due course he will meet Turner, before publishing *Modern Painters*, in defence of the artist.

But it is this birthday gift that Ruskin will later look back upon as decisive in determining his life's work, and write: 'Yet men are made what they finally become only by the external accidents which are in harmony with their inner nature.' Armed with drawing equipment and a journal, he will walk on the pier.

> *Stand on the pier and look around you. The sky is a French sky, it is a very turquoise, the sea is a French sea in everything but its want of motion, the air is French air, none of your boisterous sea puffs that blow the dust in your eyes when you wish to be particularly clear-sighted. No, it is a mere breath, you can't call it a breeze, yet bearing a delicious, a balmy coolness and a little, a very little smell of the sea.*

The Wordsworths in Calais

Picture Dorothy, aged 31, and brother William, aged 32, walking on the Calais sea-shore in the August evenings of 1802. William will be marrying Mary Hutchinson in the coming October, but they have taken the Dover ferry to meet 36-year-old Annette Vallon and William's daughter, Caroline Vallon, now nine. William had been in revolutionary France in 1791–92, to improve his French and his job prospects and Annette, in Orleans, had helped him achieve those goals. Now they were meeting again.

> *The weather was very hot. We walked by the shore-line almost every evening with Annette and Caroline or Wm and I alone. I had a bad cold and could not bathe at first but William did. It was a pretty sight to see as we walked upon the sands when the tide was low perhaps a hundred people bathing about a*

quarter of a mile distant from us, and we had delightful walks after the heat of the day was passed away – seeing far off in the west the Coast of England like a cloud crested with Dover Castle, which was but like the summit of the cloud.

So, if your ferry arrives in Calais in the late evening with a setting sun, picture the group of four on the pier, and Dorothy thinking as she gazes at the darkened shape of the wooden fort at the harbour entrance, standing on its 'pillars of Ebony,' that 'Nothing in romance was half so beautiful' and spying through those pillars in the evening sun, 'purple waves brighter than precious stones for ever melting away on the sands', and little boats rowing out of the harbour with wings of fire ... and then, as the colours fade, seeing 'the two lights of England, lighted up by the Englishmen in our country, to warn vessels of rocks and sands'.

Imagine William, too, on Calais pier, thinking, observing, and starting to compose these words in his August 1802 poem, *Fair Star of Evening*.

Fair Star of Evening, Splendour of the west,
Star of my Country! – on the horizon's brink
Thou hangest, stooping, as might seem, to sink
On England's bosom; yet well pleased to rest,
Meanwhile, and be to her a glorious crest,
Conspicuous to the Nations. Thou I think,
Shouldst be my Country's emblem; and shouldst wink,
Bright Star! with laughter on her banners, drest
In thy fresh beauty. There! that dusky spot
Beneath thee, that is England; there she lies.

Awaiting an arrival

Years later, another batchelor and poet will stand on the pier at Calais. One of his biographers, Isabel MacDonald, pictures him at the back of the crowd, craning his neck to see, yet, at the same time, invisible to the descending passengers under his wide-brimmed travelling hat. He is Matthew Arnold, 29, and in love with Frances Lucy Wightman, now descending from the ferry with her father, Judge Wightman, who has refused to sanction the marriage both desire. 'Meet no more,' he says to the 29-year-old man, soon to be appointed Inspector of Schools; 'Frances and I will continue to plan our Continental tour.'

So there he is, composing *Calais Sands*, a poem that includes the lines ...

Yet now my glance but once hath roved
O'er Calais and its famous plain;
To England's cliffs my gaze is turn'd,
On the blue strait mine eyes I strain.

Thou comest! Yes! the vessel's cloud
Hangs dark upon the rolling sea.
Oh, that yon sea-bird's wings were mine,
To win one instant's glimpse of thee!

I must not spring to grasp thy hand,
To woo thy smile, to seek thine eye;
But I may stand far off, and gaze,
And watch thee pass unconscious by,

And spell thy looks, and guess thy thoughts,
Mixt with the idlers on the pier. –

Ah, might I always rest unseen,
So I might have thee always near!

To-morrow hurry through the fields
Of Flanders to the storied Rhine!
Tonight these soft-fringed eyes shall close
Beneath one roof, my queen! with mine.

Matthew and Frances will be married within the year.

The gentle wash of the waves

Those final words of Arnold's poem speak to the hopes
of Henry VIII, on an official business trip to France. Anne
Boleyn has accompanied him on the Dover–Calais crossing
on 11th October 1532. For five years she has refused to
be his mistress. Two biographers see the Calais stay as a
seminal moment in their relationship.

That night, in the conventional room which had been
assigned to her in the castle of Calais, she opened
her arms to Henry. She humbled herself and allowed
him to possess her. The gentle wash of the waves
was audible through the windows, the tapestries
waved in the night breeze, and a dying log fire glowed
in the hearth.

Somewhere, sometime perhaps as the wind tore
through the Calais streets ... Anne at last slept with
Henry.

Does Henry come to curse the day he went to Calais
with Anne Boleyn, and reap his revenge with an act of

vicious irony? Returned to England, Henry and Anne are married on 25th January 1533, with Anne already pregnant with the future Queen Elizabeth. Three years later, Henry will have Anne executed. One record states:

> The xix of May qwene Ann Boleyn was behedyd in the Towre of London, by the hands of the hangman of Calais, with the swerde of Calais.

O the roast beef of England

And, since we are considering revenge and irony, we might also think of William Hogarth. There he is, idly sketching the main gate of Calais, as he waits for his all-too-welcome boat back home, when suddenly he is arrested, and marched before the Governor.

'An English spy!'

'No – an English artist.'

'Then prove it.'

So Hogarth draws a series of caricatures, including a scene depicting a huge piece of beef being landed for the *Lion d'Argent Inn*, with several hungry friars following it. The Governor is beguiled, yet still orders Hogarth to remain in his hotel room and, when the wind changes armed guards will escort him to the Dover-bound packet.

Humiliated – and by the French whom he detests for their 'innate insolence, covered with an affectation of politeness' and their houses 'all gilt and beshit' – he exacts his revenge with a savagely satirical picture of Calais. There is a magnificent side of beef representing robust English independence; there are the skulking, poverty stricken, priest-ridden French, for this is *Calais Gate*, also known as *O the Roast Beef of England*.

Strict order kept in Calais

Our artist friend ought to know better than to wander about the town sketching at will, and would do should he read Thomas Croyat's observations on his first visit to Calais: here is a town that takes seriously the matter of security.

> *They have a very strict order in this towne, that if any stranger of what Nation soever he be, shal be taken walking by himself, either towards their Fortresse, which they call the Rice-banke, or about the greene of the towne, he shall be apprehended by some Soldiers, and carried to the Deputy Governor, and committed to safe custody til he hath paid some fee for his ransome.*

Emma Hamilton's relief

Why is the ailing, and hopelessly in debt Emma Hamilton, 49, so relieved to enter Calais Harbour in the summer of 1814, with 14-year-old Horatia, her child – the product of that love affair with the hero of the 1805 Battle of Trafalgar? Well, dry land means the end of seasickness. More importantly, she is now free, after over a year in London's King's Bench Prison for arrested debtors.

To survive, she has sold Nelson's blood-stained coat. Horatia has stayed with her mother learning French and Italian from her. Now as the ferry enters Calais there is just a chance she, 'the victim of artful mercenary wretches' will live to see her daughter brought up. She wants no more. She is tired and ill. The scandal of the spring 1814 two-volume publication of *The Letters of Lord Nelson to Lady Hamilton* has not helped her.

Now, she hopes to see Horatia's education completed. Horatia will attend an English lady's day-school in Calais.

She learns everything – piano, harp, languages grammatically. She already reads, writes and speaks Italian, French and English, and I am teaching her German and Spanish. Music she knows, but all must yet be cultivated to perfection, and then our own language, geography, arithmetic &c. &c. she knows. We read the English, Roman, and Grecian history ...

By Christmas 1814 the money has run out again; early the following year Emma will catch pneumonia and die, on 15th January 1815, in lodgings in Rue Fraglais, Calais.

Exiles

Philip Thicknesse has earlier described Calais as 'a sort of King's bench prison' where 'the English fugitives live within the rules, and the French inhabitants make it a rule to oppress and distress them'. Now, in his *Postscript from Calais*, his malevolence goes further:

Sir,
I found in this town the very sink of France, and the asylum of whores and rogues from England, a group of English men and women ... whose necks are protected from the stretch of a halter by twenty one miles of Gallic salt water.

We know nothing of the opinion of Harriet, Countess Granville on the matter of hanging, but she takes a rather kindlier view of the English in northern France, when, on 27th February 1824, she writes to Lady Morpeth from St Omer:

> Both Calais and this place are peopled with English, slight sinners and heavy debtors, the needy and the greedy. Berkley Craven, who is settled at Calais, walked with us this morning. He says Mr. Brummell is the happiest of men, lives chiefly with the natives, and enters into all the little gossip and tittle-tattle of the place with exactly the same zest as he was wont to do in England.

That, too, is how Harriette Wilson finds him. Although never having affected friendship for the 'beau', either in his days of triumph or in his disgrace, curiosity induces her to pay him a hasty visit in Calais while her horses are being put to the carriage.

> My inquiry, 'Si Monsieur Brummell était visible?' was answered by his valet, just such a valet as one would have given the beau in the acme of his glory, bien poudré, bien cérémonieux, et bien mis, 'que Monsieur faisant sa barbe.'
>
> 'Pardon,' added the valet, seeing me about to leave my card, 'mais Monsieur reçoit, en faisant la barbe, toujours. Monsieur est à sa seconde toilette, actuellment.'
>
> I found the beau en robe de chambre de Florence, and, if one might judge from his increased embonpoint and freshness, his disgrace had not seriously affected him ... Brummell laughed, and told me that in Calais he sought only French society; because it was his decided opinion that nothing could

*be more ridiculous than the idea of a man going to
the continent, whether from necessity or choice,
merely to associate with Englishmen.*

Honneur aux Dames

France, observes William Hazlitt, is a country 'where they
give *honneur aux Dames*'. His particular liking for the
French is 'confined to their natural and unsophisticated
character.' That and their national physiognomy which,
taken at large, is 'the reflection of good temper and
humanity'. And one further thing which is decisively in
their favour – 'they do not insult or point at strangers'.

Here, perhaps, is a lesson John Mayne might take
heed of. He has arrived in Calais on 24th August 1814,
after what has been a tedious passage. Now, in the hotel
and town, he is enjoying infinite diversion observing
women of the lower class, children, shops, carriages,
horses and drivers. His *fille de chambre* gives him no
favourable impression of the sisterhood.

*She seems a perfect sample of the ugliness a
Frenchwoman may arrive at. A large-boned, shape-
less figure, with coarse skin and staring eyes, her
waist above her breasts and petticoats to her knees.
Every part of her dress is dirty but her stockings,
which are particularly white.*

John Barber Scott, on the other hand, stuck in Calais
in a high and adverse wind on Sunday 23rd October 1814,
has arrived at a quite different judgement:

*I must confess that the walk and air of a
Frenchwoman is far more feminine and delicate than*

that of the daughters of Albion; but the latter bear the palm in prettiness of face and in delicacy of thought. If only the English damsels had the feet and ankles, sparkling eyes and easy walk of the French, they would be faultless.

Zachary Macaulay is also struck by comparisons in the appearance of English and French women: the French 'swelled out with an enormity of petticoat' while the English women 'make themselves as ridiculously slim and angular, every part of the shape being made obtrusively visible'. And nothing can match 'the freshness of the English complexion, and the beautiful smoothness of the skin'. But then, their walk:

The French women, with all the immense convexity of petticoat, and of the flowing cloaks which in this weather wrap them from head to foot, have a legerete and buoyancy in their tread, and a steadiness in their carriage, approaching to elegance, of which our women know nothing. They have not learned to walk.

That, at any rate, is what he writes to tell Mrs Macaulay in December 1823.

And Leigh Hunt, whose periodical, *Examiner,* has introduced such romantic poets as Keats and Shelley to the public cannot help thinking that the countenances of French women announce 'more pleasantness and reasonableness of intercourse, than those of my fair and serious countrywomen'. This is, of course, 'without disparagement to the angel faces which you meet with in England'. Nevertheless:

The Frenchwoman looked as if she wished to please you at any rate, and to be pleased herself. She is too conscious; and her coquetry is said, and I believe with truth, to promise more than an Englishman would easily find her to perform; but at any rate she thinks of you somehow, and is smiling and good-humoured.

And, then, their walk!

Could you not 'indicate' to our English ladies the way to walk ... how infinitely superior is the Frenchwoman's brisk springy step (albeit caused by a most plebian and un-English want of causeways) to the languid sauntering gait of most English dames!

Garrick on French bugs

We cannot be certain about David Garrick's opinion of the comparative merits of French and English women – he has, after all, married an Austrian – but he has much enjoyed his French jaunt in July 1851 and, on his return to London, even has a good word to say for French bed-bugs in his letter to his 'Dear and very good friend', the gout-ridden, Revd Dr John Hoadly:

I thank thee most heartily for thy kind & friendly Letter – I am return'd with my better half, safe & sound from Paris & as true an Englishman as Ever – not but let me tell thee, (thou reverend Son of a – more reverend Father), I am much, very much pleas'd with my Jaunt, & am ready & willing to take ye Same & for a Month longer, whenever Business will

permit & I am call'd upon – I am sorry that son of a
Bitch ye Gout, likes the tenement so well, that there's
now routing him from thy Plump Body; the Bugs in
France would be glad to see thee there, & many a
delicious Meal they would make of thee; Beef &
Pudding, tho at second hand, is a great rarity, &
therefore Thou art a Feast fit for the Bugs!

Hester Piozzi leaves her mark in Calais

Nor do we know anything of Hester Piozzi's gait. We do,
however, know that, back in her Calais hotel at the end
of her 30-month second honeymoon which started in
Dover in September 1784, she has left these lines for
future travellers.

Over Mountains, Rivers, Valleys,
Here are we return'd to Calais;
After all their Taunts and Malice,
Entering safe the Gates of Calais:
While constrain'd our Captain dallies
Waiting for a Wind at Calais,
Wandring Muse! prepare some Sallies
To divert Ennui at Calais. –
Turkish Ships, Venetian Gallies,
Have We seen since last at Calais,
But tho' Hogarth – Rogue who raillies
Ridicules the French at Calais,
We who have walked o'er many a Palace,
Quite well content return to Calais:
For, striking honestly the Tallies,
There's little Choice 'twixt them and Calais.

So Adieu to la Belle France, and Welcome Merry England

However anxious you may be to begin the final stage of the journey home, the same capricious, unpredictable winds that held you up in Dover can delay you again. So 15-year-old Charles Petty (son of Sir William, inventor of the Double-Bottom ship) discovers in October 1687.

I went alone through Dunkirk and Gravelines to Calais, where staying some dayes for a wind, I att last mett with a bad one, which kept us 18 houres at sea, Split our Top Saile, and made the sea break often over our Sterne, and when it should have brought us into Dover, turned Calme. Soe as the sea both goeing and coming proved to mee a Schooll of Navigation wherein I was well whipt!

Horace Walpole's return to England is similarly delayed. Stuck in his Calais hotel, he bangs the words down on paper with venom: 'Is the wind laid? Shall I never get aboard?' It is Friday, 11th September 1741, and he has been in Calais two days, already, and still the tempest blows. Furthermore, there has been trouble with the Customs: opening his trunk, they would have confiscated his medals, but 'with much ado and much three louis's [d'or] they let them pass'. He will not get away till tomorrow morning:

I came over in a yacht with East India captains'
widows, a Catholic girl coming from a convent to be
married, with an Irish priest to guard her, who says
he studied medicines for two years, and after that
he studied learning for two years more.

A perplexed 22-year-old waits for a favourable wind
June 1785, and Miss Berry is also waiting for a favourable
wind. She is just 22, and at the end of a two-year
European tour with her father and her younger sister,
Agnes. Their mother (dead from milk fever since 1767)
had wanted for her daughter not good looks, but, rather,
'a vigorous understanding'.

Her heart-broken father had abandoned the world
and Miss Berry was soon to find that 'I had to lead those
who ought to have led me; that I must be a protecting
mother, instead of a gay companion to my sister; and to
my father a guide and monitor instead of finding in him
a tutor and protector.'

Now we find her sitting at Dessein's in Calais – her
first European tour at an end – waiting for the favourable wind that will return her to Dover, perplexed by her
own feelings.

My travels are over, then. Here I am at the extremity
of France, I can see from far off the shores of my
native country, three hours with a favourable wind
and I shall be there. But where are those sweet
sensations, those tears of joy, that deep and tender
feeling that I have always hoped to experience at a
moment which should have always been dear to me?
I am not experiencing them. You are not experiencing

them! Unhappy! And why? How could you have lost the most sweet, the most natural, the most delicious of all raptures? You have lost it! And what have you gained in its place? A sad assurance that happiness does not come from any country, that its essence exists in ourselves and that you do not have it; that your proud soul, your excessive sensitivity have destroyed it; that you have lost the amiable weaknesses, the endearing mistakes, the happy presumptions of your age and sex, without having acquired that strength of soul, those sure and extended rays of light – in short, that superior virtue which alone can dispense with pleasures and is alone capable of elevating our souls to the level of its own grandeur, knowing how to make itself loved even by those who do not resemble it … I speak frankly to you because I love you, I know that Nature has enriched you with all its gifts, I recall your childhood, I know your heart, I perceived its origin, the source of all its mistakes. You are still capable of much; I wish to restore you to yourself, pluck you from the precipice towards which you are heading, to save you from this terrible apathy, to which your mistakes, your spirit, your very sensitivity are leading you.

Quelle vie

See Ann, Lady Fanshawe, aged 41, on board a little French man-of-war, now making its way out of Calais harbour on 11th November 1666. Her children are on board with her: Katherine, fourteen; Margaret, thirteen; Ann, eleven; Elizabeth, four; and one-year-old Richard. So, too, is her husband's coffin on this Dover-bound ferry.

She has time, on the journey home, to contemplate her children who are not with her: Harrison would have been twenty-one, but died in Oxford after two weeks; Ann, born in Jersey, would have been twenty – 'a girl whose beauty and wit exceeded all that I ever saw of her age,' said her mother – but who died aged nine at Tankersley Park in Yorkshire; Henry would have been nineteen, but died aged two; Richard would have been eighteen, but died aged eleven; Elizabeth would have been seventeen but died of a fever in Madrid just ten days old; and the second Elizabeth would have been fifteen, but died aged five; and Mary would have been ten, but died aged four; and Henry would have been nine, but died aged one year old; and Richard would have been three, but died aged a few months.

Quelle vie. My husband has had six sons and eight daughters borne and christened and I have miscarried of six more.

There will be time, also, to think of the places she has lived in during the 22 years of her married life. She runs through those she can remember, in order: Oxford, Bristol, Penzance, Scilly Isles, Jersey, Caen, London, France again, London, Paris, England (via Calais in a great storm, with the boat half full of water); then on to Cork, Limerick, Galway; then to Malaga, Madrid, San Sebastián, and Paris; then to London, Bayfordbury (Herts), Tankersley Park (Yorkshire), Frognal (Kent), Bengey (Herts), Bath, Ware, London; then via Calais in disguise to Paris, on to London again, then Paris, Brussels, London, Hertford, London; then, after her husband, a devoted Royalist, is appointed Ambassador – first to Portugal then

Spain – there is Lisbon, London, Madrid, and now coming home to London again, with her embalmed husband in his coffin on the boat, now clear of Calais harbour and out into the Channel.

Chateaubriand returns as Ambassador

Chateaubriand, newly appointed Ambassador to Britain, is returning to a country he knew as a miserably impoverished refugee from the Revolution some twenty years earlier. But now he must write to the two women whose intercessions on his behalf have helped secure him this diplomatic plum: first, to the Duchesse de Duras, friend, confidante and patroness, who has been pleading to see him before his departure from Paris on 1st April 1822:

In stirring times it is a mistake to make friends of ambassadors if you would not have them embroiled in matters of state. The only moment at which I am free to see you is after dinner, at eight o'clock and, even then, only for an instant, since I leave tonight.

Then to his present mistress, Mme de Récamier, reputedly 'the loveliest woman of her age':

Don't be too sad, my sweet angel. I love you; I'll always love you. I shall never change. I'll write to you. I'll come back quickly and as soon as you order it. It won't last all that long, and then I'll be with you for ever! Good night. I'll write from Calais the day after tomorrow.

In Calais, on 3rd April, he also writes again to Mme de Duras, whom he refers to as his 'sister'. No doubt her unrequited love for him will allow her, once more, to smile indulgently at his egoism and pride.

Here I am in Calais, a town I travelled through 22 years ago. You cannot imagine how I feel when I reflect on what has happened to me since those days and when I think of the destiny which sends me back as an Ambassador to a country which I left as a poor émigré, completely unknown and so wretched. Yet I am not devoid of pride for having brought about such a destiny. I owe it only to what I was then, as I came through this place ... The star of the traveller is following me.

And what of Mme de Chateaubriand? She will stay in Paris. Her husband's extravagant account of the awfulness of the English weather has dissuaded her of any wish she might have had to accompany him to the London Embassy.

So, Chateaubriand travels alone, and travels with gay abandon on the rough, eleven-hour crossing to Dover. He sings; he climbs the mast; he laughs at his seasick fellow passengers, and he revels in his own change of fortune.

From Dover, on 5th April, he writes again to Mme de Récamier:

You can see that I've crossed the sea. I'll be in London this evening. I'll write to you. I cannot see myself in this country without heart-ache. I was so wretched there and so young then.

And again from London on 9th April:

I do so much need to receive a line from you. I wrote to you from Calais and from Dover. I am here in London where I have only truly sad memories and where I am so alone, in spite of what you think and say ... I am waiting for a note from you; you never write more than a few words.

But Mme de Récamier is in no hurry to reply. Does she already know that the old *roué* will not be wretched this time, nor alone, for there will be an abundance of ladies to erase his sad memories? Is she beginning to resent all the other madams, the other 'sweet angels'? Perhaps, for in a year's time she will flee to Italy to sever the relationship, just as Mme de Duras will retire to die, alone, in Nice.

Yet now, as Chateaubriand rediscovers his youth spent as a mariner, and prances about the pitching deck of the ferry taking him to a glittering life in London, can he imagine that it will be Mme de Récamier, white-haired and near-blind, who will sit in almost solitary vigil at his deathbed, while the explosions of the 1848 Revolution rattle the window panes?

Fenimore Cooper returns to England.
The American writer, Fenimore Cooper, reports that the Calais quay is crowded with clamorous porters, while the *gendarmes* keep an eye to the police regulations, lest a stray rogue, more or less, might pass undetected between the two great capitals of Europe. 'It helped boarding the ferry if you came from one of the Calais hotels, for one

of the hotel commissionaires would accompany you and see your problems minimised.'

Entering the ferry from the quay depends upon the state of the tide – this is 1828, remember. Fenimore Cooper has to get down a ladder of some fifteen steps into the boat, because 'the rise and fall of the water is so great, in these high narrow seas, that vessels are sometimes on a level with the quays, and at others three or four fathoms below them'.

> *It is possible to see across the Straits of Dover, in clear weather, but, on this occasion, we had nothing visible before us, but an horizon of water, as we paddled through the long entrance of the little haven, into the North Sea. The day was calm, and, an unusual circumstance in swift tides and narrow passages, the channel was as smooth as a pond. Even the ground swell was too gentle to disturb the omelettes of M. Dessein's successor ... After a run of two hours, the cliffs of Dover became distinctly visible.*

We are left to speculate about how this one-time merchant–mariner passes the time on that smooth-watered February crossing before the cliffs of Dover become visible. He is, of course, a writer of sea stories now, stories like *The Pilot* and *Red Rover*. Is it possible, then, that he rehearses how his characters might talk about the sea on such a day? 'There is not enough wind to blow a lady's curl aside.'

And asked which way the wind is blowing, a sailor up aloft replies – 'We feel a light cat's-paw, now and then, from the land, Sir, but our topsail hangs in the clew lines, Sir, without winking.' Is this the langauge of a mariner?

Break a secret to mother

Maria Edgeworth, also a novelist (admired by Jane Austen), and a co-author, with her father, of *Practical Education* which has carried Jean Rousseau's ideas on pedagogy across the Channel, smiles as the boat makes headway out of Calais on 6th December 1820. This is better than the steamboat crossing from Dublin to Holyhead at the start of her memorable tour to Europe, when 'the jigging motion of the Holyhead steamer is like the shake felt in a carriage when a pig is scratching himself against the hind wheel while waiting at an Irish inn door'.

Her didactic letter to Lucy, written in Calais, is also now on its way to Dublin, and the instructions that it contains are clear:

Lucy, find a good time to break a secret to mother. She must not be too busy. Her mind is to be at ease. Then start. Tell her I know she and my brother Lovell have much confidence in me. Tell them I am bringing home a French washerwoman. But she will give no trouble. She will cost nothing. She is a sourde et muette. Tell mother, until a place is found for her, she can sleep in mother's dressing-room. Now stop, and wait five minutes. Listen to what everyone has to say. Then say, 'Well, if no better place can be found for my washerwoman, she may stand on mother's chimney-piece!'

Should you happen to see a white sail ...
Picture in your mind Mary Shelley's boat leaving Calais, on 25th August 1823, into a glassy sea: she, relieved and calm, no violent, wind-pummelled sea to activate her powerful imagination, the imagination that has created the novel *Frankenstein, or the Modern Prometheus;* beside her sits her son, Percy Florence ('Persino'), aged four; the sea is smooth and in the distance, Dover.

Memories come of her departure in March 1918 with son, William, and Percy Byssche. Now both are dead – William from malaria in Rome and Percy Byssche drowned off the Italian coast with his friend Edward Williams but a year ago – and she alone, now, with Percy Florence. 'He is my all. I could not live a day without my boy.'

But there is no sense of home-coming for Mary, no keen anticipation. 'England! what a fearful sound! – best I submit.' Safeguarding Persino's financial future has made necessary, even if reluctantly, the Calais journey away from her blessed and beloved Italy – the land whose sky 'canopies the tombs of my lost treasures. I return to the dreariest reality ...'

The widowed dreamer, she welcomes now her aloneness. The balm? Persino and study. Her opiate? 'The exercise of my mind, the improvement of my understanding and the acquirement of knowledge.' And what else? She looks forward to the grave with hope. Her heart, till then, will be beneath that weed-grown wall in Rome, where her husband's ashes are laid. Solitary walks give her consolation now. And, on one such walk, earlier in the spring of the year, she catches sight of a white sail. Is it Percy Byssche, and Edward Williams, returned from the sea?

*I saw the other day a white sail at a distance, and
with a kind of madness of deception, I thought there
they are! I will take a boat and go out to them.*

Picture, then, Mary Shelley leaving Calais. And should
you happen to see a white sail coming towards you,
think of Mary on the crossing. But maybe you won't
have time to do that, for you might be reading her 1818
novel, *Frankenstein*.

*We took our passage ... and sailed with a fair wind.
It was midnight. I lay on the deck looking at the
stars, and listening to the dashing of the waves ...
the past appeared to me in the light of a frightful
dream; yet the vessel in which I was, the wind that
blew me ... and the sea which surrounded me told
me too forcibly that I was deceived by no vision,
and that Clerval, my friend and dearest companion,
had fallen a victim to me and the monster of my
creation.*

Revd William Cole and the chamber-pot

It is 2.00 p.m. on Monday, 2nd December 1765 – a fine
day in Calais with an excessive hard frost. Revd William
Cole of Blecheley, now returning from his visit to the
Catholic College of Louis le Grand, together with his
servant and 40 other passengers, boards the Dover ferry
at high water. Passengers include 'Messrs Mills and their
Blacks', a French gentleman wearing the Cross of St Lewis
and 'several other French people of a meaner quality'.
Beside his 'box & portmanteaus', William has a cold
partridge and bread for the passage. And more:

I had also a Hare, a Brace of Woodcocks & a Woodcock Pye in a Basket, & 3 Bottles of Beaune Wine, or Burgundy, which I had brought with me from Paris, & a Neat's Tongue or two, thinking to have eaten them on the Road, with the Wine: but as I never touched them, I got the Mate of the Ship, to whom I gave a Guinea, to take Care of these Things, with 2 or 3 other Bottles of Ratify from Boulogne, with the Parcels I had from Mr Walpole, with many Trinkets of my own, & some Books & Things of no great Consequence which might have been stopped at the Custom House at Dover, & put them aside, & bring them to me, when I was ashore: which he did very faithfully by little at a Time: my Box & Portmanteaus being sent to the Custom House by my Servant, where I paid about 5 Shillings Duty for a few Things which were in them.

The sea is beautiful, not too rough, and the sun shines till its setting, but William is prepared for the colder night air with an additional 'Great Coat and a good glass of Brandy from Barber, the ship's mate'. The passengers are on deck, where there is a deal of immoderate laughter. The cause of all the jollity is a French kitchen maid, travelling in the entourage* of Lord and Lady St George, who has taken to Revd Cole's servant and sits close by him.

Then, realising that William is a reverend, she announces that in the case of any danger, she would

---

* Their six-year-old daughter, a young French girl as companion to her, an English footman, a male French cook, a French Governante, an Irish Lady's Maid, and 'an ordinary French woman, who was to be under the Cook in the kitchen'.

depend upon him for assistance; she also indicates that she would like to eat and drink. Revd Cole sees to it that she has a loaf and a little French brandy. Now a problem arises for her. She cannot speak English, but knows that he speaks French. As Revd Cole confides in his journal:

She desired me to beg one of the Sailors to give her a Chamber Pot: upon which, thinking she was sick, as many were upon the Deck, I advised her to go to the Side of the Ship, & my Servant should hold her by her Gown for Fear of tumbling over Board: but she directly told me, that however practicable a Situation might be for us, it would not suit her at all; & without more ado, or further Ceremony, sans facon, a la francoise, she plainly told me she wanted a Chamber Pot, pour faire lacher l'Eau; these were her Words; so I forthwith got her accommodated with one, which she with as little Shame as Decency and Ceremony made immediate use of, before all the Company, and then gave it with the utmost Sangfroid and Indifference to my Servant to empty it over Board for her: while the Irish Maid was crying out 'Jesu Maria' and the two other Maids quite unabashed by the Woman's Impudence. I observed her Ladyship took no Notice, but seemed thoroughly vexed and chagrined at such Indecency, and I guess, would not take her with her to Ireland upon this Account: for my servant told me he saw her at Dover, after all the other Part of the Family were gone for London. The Woman, when she saw me and some others of the Company laughing at her Action, talked reasonably and sensibly upon the Occasion, as any one could: asked in plain, gras, and indelicate words, what any of us would do, if a sudden Griping should take us and we should want to go to the Necessary House. But tho' the woman's Argument's were right in the main, yet she mistook only in this single very material Point: that altho' what she had done was absolutely necessary, yet she might have made an Excuse to have gone under Deck & have done privately, & by herself, what she chose to do before all the World. But such is the difference between English and French Education and Customs! We carry to an Excess our Delicacy in these Matters, while our Neighbours exceed in the other offensive Extreme. A proper Medium would certainly be the Best.

Miss Berry and Fanny Burney pass each other

On the evening of Wednesday, 14th April 1802, Miss Berry arrives in Calais to catch a ferry home. In Paris she has been to the theatre, and there encountered for herself the influence of the Revolution.

We were shown into a box au premier rang, where only one man of very ordinary appearance was sitting in the front row. We supposed he would offer us his place, mais point de tout, he did not even look towards us; he never even made the least movement by way of inviting us to sit beside him. This is indeed a revolution in France, and such a one as I could not have believed if I had not seen it! We sat for a time behind our man, who, to complete the business, chewed tobacco, and at every instant spat into the empty place beside him.

The journey from Paris has not been without its share of problems.

No sooner were we on our way than the postilion fell off one of the horses. The crowd said he was drunk. That delayed us; the next day (Monday) an iron on the carriage broke at Clermont; that was repaired and broke again the next day near Pecquigny.

Arriving at Calais the wind is contrary, and remains so throughout Thursday. Only on the following day will she be able to leave for Dover.

Went on board the 'Swift'; sailed from Calais Pier a quarter after eleven: fine day, but the wind fell almost entirely. At seven o'clock in the evening we were within five miles of Dover in a dead calm; got into a Dover boat, were rowed into the harbour, and arrived at the York Hotel at a quarter after eight, having been just nine hours on our passage.

Friday, 16th April 1802 is also the day Fanny Burney leaves Dover to rejoin her previously exiled husband. Had she been able to rise from her sick-bed during that ghastly twenty-hour voyage she might have seen Miss Berry descending from Captain Baxter's ferry five miles out. Perhaps Adrienne, skipping about the deck, did.

In sight of the white cliffs

In the summer of 1808, Benjamin Haydon looks back at the French coastline where, he thinks, Bonaparte stood 'with disappointment and malice', surveying the cliffs of England. Then, half-way across the Channel, he turns to face England.

> *I never saw any coast so exactly answering the feeling excited by Homer's description and scenery; here was the Place to read Homer ... I almost thought I saw Achilles in naked majesty moving his "mighty thighs" along the Shore.*

And, after an absence of two years travelling in France and Italy, Tobias Smollett is finally able to indulge his view with a sight of Britain, and 'Dear Sir, you cannot imagine what pleasure I feel while I survey the white cliffs of Dover, at this distance.'

As his vessel nears home, there is still time to reflect upon that pleasure.

> *Not that I am at all affected by the nescia qua dulcedine natalis soli, of Horace. That seems to be a kind of fanaticism founded on the prejudices of education, which induces a Laplander to place the terrestrial paradise among the snows of Norway, and a Swiss to prefer the barren mountains of Solleure to the fruitful plains of Lombardy. I am attached to my country, because it is the land of liberty, cleanliness and convenience: but I love it still more tenderly, as the scene of all my interesting connexions; as the habitation of my friends, for whose conversation, correspondence and esteem, I wish alone to live.*

On being back in England

Returning to England on that fine February day in 1828 aboard the English steam-packet, chosen in preference to the French 'from a latent distrust of Gallic seamanship', Fenimore Cooper is inclined to make comparisons.

If we were struck with the contrast between England and France, on first reaching the latter country, I think we were still more so on returning to the former. Four hours before we were in the region of politeness, vociferation, snatching, fun and fraud, on the quay of Calais; and now we were in that of quiet, sulkiness, extortion, thank'ees and half crowns, on that of Dover.

Grateful to be an Englishman

Fenimore Cooper is an American, but Joseph Farington is an Englishman and thankful for it as he, too, is struck by the contrasts there are to be observed on his return in October 1802.

I felt on my return a difference the most striking; it was expressed in everything; and may be explained by saying that it was coming from disorder to order. From Confusion, to convenience: from subjection to freedom. I no longer saw the people covered with the patches of necessity, or the ridiculous mixtures of frippery imitations of finery with the coarse clothing of poverty. All appeared appropriate and substantial, and every man seemed respectable because his distinct & proper Character was consistently maintained. What must be the nature of that mind that would not feel grateful that it was his Lot to be an Englishman; a man entitled from his Birth to participate in such advantages as in no other country can be found.

Lady Glenbervie's health

At 5.30 a.m. on 14th August 1816, in the *Rose Inn*, Sittingbourne, Lord Glenbervie is able to write in his diary:

Lady Glenbervie has shown great, the greatest, delight at finding herself returned to her dear country and so near seeing her sisters, and has not said half what I know she feels. There was all yesterday a manifest and striking change in her countenance and spirits, and the ease and haleness of her voice all day yesterday. When she did sleep her sleep was easier and more natural ... and she ate a hearty breakfast à la fourchette at the 'Ship' about 12 o'clock and a more hearty souper at about 9 at this inn of the 'Rose'.

Lord Glenbervie's optimistic diary account of his wife's health is natural. Much has preceded it to cause him worry. In Naples, on 16th March, Lady Glenbervie is struck 'with an almost total cessation of pulse, coldness of the limbs and loss of recollection'. She is bled in the arm, but there are more attacks. Leeches are applied behind her ears, and she is given doses of manna, senna and salts. So imagine him, now, sitting up in bed in The Rose, browsing through his diary entries on their return from Naples with his dear Kitty.

May 30, Terni: This begins our third day's journey from Rome, and Lady Glenbervie seems to have borne it as well as that from Naples, except that she is more frequently, and for longer spaces of time, drowsy, I hope from the laudanum. Her room is at this time so quiet that I flatter myself she has had a good night.

June 11, Florence: She has slept tolerably, but is now feverish, low, and short-breathed.

June 15, Bologna: My dear Kitty on the whole as well as could be expected.

June 16, Bologna: Lady Glenbervie had a very tolerable night.

July 9, Geneva: She has, thank God, at this moment (3.00 am), been in a quiet and sound sleep for four or five hours.

July 11, Geneva: A wretched night. Her son and her maid are with her (5.00am), and I have heard from the outside of the door her son reading the service of the sick to her, or some prayers she has selected in Taylor's 'Holy Dying'. She has twice tonight taken in all twelve drops of laudanum.

July 16, 4.15 a.m., in bed, Geneva: I wakened about half-past three, and soon after heard Lady Glenbervie speaking a little, but very quietly, and she very soon ceased.

July 23, 5.30 a.m., in bed, Val de Suzon: I thought I heard Lady Glenbervie, who is in the opposite room, about half an hour ago, (5.00am), but on listening at her door, I found everything quiet.

July 24, Montbard: I think she went to bed about eleven and everything is at present very quiet in her room.

At the end of July they are in Paris where, Glenbervie confides to his diary, 'the feelings and reflections which naturally crowded upon her, on commencing this last great stage of our long journey, oppressed her poor exhausted spirits, and produced a fit of crying and afterwards of religious and awful forebodings, most affecting and painful to me'. Then:

August 7, 2.30 p.m., Amiens: We arrived here at half past one after a short journey of three and a half posts, in a fine but cloudy day. Lady Glenbervie was remarkably well.
August 8, 5.30 p.m., Abbeville: Lady Glenbervie says that she has not felt so well for many days.
August 11, 10.30 p.m., in bed, Calais: Lady Glenbervie had an excellent night, and has been particularly well all day.
August 12, 4.10 a.m., Calais: It has just begun to dawn. If the wind proves fair, and the sea smooth ... we embark at 7.

But the morning proves unpromising and at 11 o'clock Captain Barnet of the packet they have hired, the *Ant*, decides that the wind is too high to get a passage today.

August 13, 3.00 a.m., in bed. Calais. Joseph has just wakened me from a sound sleep. He says the morning is fine. I am going to get up immediately.

At which point Lord Glenbervie closes his diary. The morning is fine and they will embark from the pier at Calais at half-past four and, after a favourable passage, though in foggy, drizzling weather, but 'without once backing or shifting the sails, or the slightest tossing of the vessel', they will be in the *Ship Inn*, Dover, that evening. The next entry, recalling his wife's better health, will be written in Sittingbourne.

Dover customs-house

Joseph Farington has had very little trouble with the customs officials. To be sure, some painting brushes he has brought over from France are initially detained, but when he returns to the customs-house the following morning 'we found them disposed to let our Brushes pass witht. paying duty as being articles of little value'.

Mrs Thrale, however, fears them. In the comfort of Dessein's at the end of her Paris venture, when 'poor Sam [Johnson] seems happy that he is at least within Sight of England', she reports in her journal:

> *Custom House Officers indeed I have a dread of yet, though a three Livre piece has hitherto silenced the most sullen, but at Dover we are threatened with sad brutal Fellows – Nous verrons.*

In fact, we don't see: she makes no further mention of the Dover customs-house officers – so we need not assume the worst.

But these same officers serve to mar the pleasure of John Mayne's return to England on 8th March 1815.

> *It gave me such a feeling of happiness to be in my own country again, with English faces and English voices about me, that I was disposed to admire although everything had not, indeed, been truly*

admirable. On the road to town every carriage, every horse, every house, and every person was interesting, and my attention was as completely engaged as it ever had been in a strange country where every object was wholly new.

Fortunately for my safety, and for that of other English travellers who return to their native land with my feelings, Dover and its customs-house are most judiciously placed in the way, to counteract the effects of a too excessive joy. We found them most effectual dampers, for after having been forced to pay half-a-guinea each for a boat to carry us ten yards, we were almost suffocated and pressed into the sand upon the beach by a crowd of noisy ruffians, who would have forced us to lodge that night in five hotels at the same time; and having escaped this danger, we were stretched upon the rack of the custom-house, and, finally, cheated at our inn more than we had ever been in France or Italy.

The Earl of Albemarle has also had his difficulties with Customs. Arriving back at Dover in December 1815, with the Third Battalion of the Fourteenth Foot ('mainly Buckinghamshire lads fresh from the plough') he finds everyone, post-Waterloo, ignores them. Everyone, that is, but the custom-house officers, particularly alert because a brigade of artillery with guns loaded to their muzzle with French lace has slipped through their fingers the previous day.

At landing, a scuffle ensued between Lord Lowther, who had a red Treasury box in his hand, and the Custom House officers, and my friend Grattan, who had a little deal box under his arm. Lowther was dispossessed of his box and pushed down. Grattan drew his sword-stick. The Duke, Robert Milnes and myself, put ourselves into sparring attitudes, but the affray terminated without coming to blows ... Lowther prudently forbore to strike; he recollected folks having been trounced for resisting the delegates of the Douane; but he and the Duke of Leinster, Milnes, and myself, trotted off to Stowe, the collector, who received the peers with the utmost civility, but told me it was impossible to know men of rank coming in an open boat.

Home

William Hazlitt does not let us know how he has fared at the customs-house – he's unlikely to be loaded with French lace – but, as we might anticipate, he is still in grumbling mood when he returns to Dover in October 1825.

The beef-steak which you order ... with patriotic yearnings for its reputation is accordingly filled with ciders – the muton is done to a rag – the soup not eatable – the porter sour – the bread gritty – the butter rancid ... In the midst of all this ill fare you meet with equally bad treatment. While you are trying to digest a tough beef-steak, a fellow comes in and peremptorily demands your fare.

Sir Walter Scott, on the other hand, is enjoying his hot lunch in Dover on 9th November 1826, after a slow passage on a raw, cold day with a surly and contrary wind and tide. He concludes his diary entry:

*So adieu to la belle France and wellcome Merry
England.*

And always, even now, there is the uncertainty of
timing. Mrs Thrale, reaches home on 11th November 1775.

*We returned to Dover with Captain Baxter, who was
much disturbed by Fears lest we should lose the Tide
& be obliged to sleep on Shipboard or hazard some
chance – I never knew what – by coming on Shore
in a Boat. However we saved our Tide as the phrase
is by 4 Minutes only, & all was to our wish ...*

And, with everything to her wish, Mrs Hester Thrale is
able to conclude her French journal.

*My Adventures are now at an End
& so shall be my Journal.*

Finished at Dover

Saturday – 11th November 1775.

References

Adams, H., *The Letters of Mrs. Henry Adams*, edited by
W. Thoron, Little, Brown and Co., 1936

Anderson, E., *The Letters of Mozart and his Family*,
Macmillan, 1938

Berry, M., *The Journals and Correspondence of Mary
Berry*, 1865

Burke, E., *Correspondence of the Right Hon. Edmund
Burke*, 1844

Burney, F., *Diary and Letters of Madame D'Arblay*,
edited by C. Barrett, Swan Sonnenschein, 1893

Callow, W., *William Callow: an Autobiography*, edited by
H. M. Cundall, Adam and Charles Black, 1908

Carlyle, T., *The Love Letters of Thomas Carlyle and Jane
Welsh*, edited by A. Carlyle, John Lane, 1909

Chateaubriand, *Correspondance Général*, edited by
P. Riberette, Société Chateaubriand

Clairmont, C., *The Journals of Claire Clairmont*, edited
by M. K. Stocking, Harvard University Press, 1968

Coke, M., *Letters and Journals of Lady Mary Coke*, 1863

Cole, W., *A Journal of my Journey to Paris in the Year
1765*, edited by F. G. Stokes, Constable, 1931

Cooper, J. F., *Cooper's Gleanings in Europe: England*,
edited by R. Spiller, Oxford University Press, 1928

Croyat, T., *Coryat's Crudities*, MacLehose, 1905 (first
published 1611)

Dibdin, T. F., *A Bibliographical Antiquarian and
Picturesque Tour in France and Germany*, 1829

Dickens, C., 'Science at Sea' in *Household Words*,
Volume III, 1851

Edgeworth, M., *Life and Letters of Maria Edgeworth*, 1894

Evelyn, J., *The Diary of John Evelyn* edited by E. S. de Beer, Oxford University Press, 1955

Fanshawe, Lady, *The Memories of Ann Lady Fanshawe*, edited by H. C. Fanshawe, Bodley Head, 1907

Farington, J., *The Farington Diary*, edited by J. Grieg, Hutchinson, 1923

Garrick, D., *The Letters of David Garrick*, edited by D. M. Little and G. M. Kahrl, Oxford University Press, 1963

Gibbon, E., *The Letters of Edward Gibbon*, edited by J. E. Norton, Cassell, 1956

Glenbervie, Lord, *The Diaries of Sylvester Douglas (Lord Glenbervie)*, edited by F. Bickley, Constable, 1928

Granville, Duchess, *Letters of Harriet, Countess Granville, 1810–1845*, Longmans, Green & Co., 1894

Haydn, J., *The Collected Correspondence and London Notebooks of Joseph Haydn*, edited by H. C. Landon, Barrie & Jenkins, 1959

Haydon, B. R., *Autobiography and Memoirs of Benjamin Robert Haydon*, edited by T. Taylor, Peter Davies, 1926

Hazlitt, W., *Notes of a Journey Through France and Italy*, 1826

Hobhouse, H., *The Diary of Henry Hobhouse*, edited by A. Aspinall, Home and Van Thal, 1947

Hoby, Lady Elizabeth, *Callender of State Papers (Dom.) Addenda 1566–1579*

Hopkins, G. M., *The Note-Books and Papers of Gerard Manley Hopkins*, edited by H. House, Oxford University Press, 1937

Hunt, L., 'English and French Females' in *Essays and Sketches*, edited by A. Symonds, J. M. Dent, 1905

Jameson, Mrs., *The Diary of an Ennuyée*, 1826

Johnson, S., *The French Journals of Mrs Thrale and Dr. Johnson*, edited by M. Tyson and H. Guppy, Manchester University Press, 1932

von La Roche, S., *Sophie in London 1786, being the diary of Sophie von La Roche*, translated by C. Williams, Jonathan Cape, 1933

Latouche, J., *Travels in Portugal*, 1875

Macaulay, Z., *Life and Letters of Zachary Macaulay*, edited by Viscountess Knutsford, Edward Arnold, 1900

Malmesbury, Earl, *Diaries and Correspondence of James Harris, First Earl of Malmesbury*, 1844

Manning, T., *The Letters of Thomas Manning to Charles Lamb*, Martin Secker, 1925

Mayne, J., *The Journal of John Mayne*, Colles, 1909

Mill, J. S., *John Mill's Boyhood Visit to France*, edited by A. J. Mill, University of Toronto Press, 1960

Montagu, E., *Mrs Montagu, 'Queen of the Blues': Her Letters and Friendships from 1762–1800*, edited by R. Blunt, Constable, 1932

Montagu, Lady, *The Letters and Works of Lady Mary Wortley Montagu*, edited by Lord Wharncliffe, 1837

Palmer, S., *The Letters of Samuel Palmer*, edited by R. Lister, Oxford University Press, 1974

Petty, C., *The Petty–Southwell Correspondence, 1670–1687*, edited by the Marquis of Lansdowne, Constable, 1928

Piozzi, H. L., *Autobiography, Letters and Literary Remains of Mrs Piozzi*, edited by A. Hayward, 1861

Prévost, Abbé, *Mémoires d'un Homme de Qualité*

Ruskin, J., *The Works of Ruskin*, edited by E. T. Cook
and A. Wedderburn, George Allen, 1903

Scott, J. B., *An Englishman at Home and Abroad,
1792–1828: extracts from the diaries of J. B. Scott
of Bungay, Suffolk*, edited by Ethel Mann, Heath
Cranton, 1930

Scott, W., *The Journal of Sir Walter Scott, 1825–26*,
edited by J. G. Tait, Oliver and Boyd, 1939

Shelley, M., *The Journals of Mary Shelley, 1814–1844*,
edited by P. R. Feldman and D. Scott-Kilvert, Oxford
University Press, 1987

Shelley, P. B., *The Letters of Percy Byssche Shelley*,
edited by R. Ingpen, Pitman, 1909

Smollett, T., *Travels Through France and Italy*, 1766

Sterne, L., *The Life and Opinion of Tristram Shandy,
Gentleman*, 1760

Sterne, L., *A Sentimental Journey through France and
Italy*, 1768

Stevenson, S. W., *Journal of a Tour through Part of
France, Flanders and Holland*, Norfolk Chronicle
Press, 1817

Surtees, R. S., *Jorrock's Jaunts and Jollities*, Methuen,
1903

Thackeray, W., *The Book of Snobs*, 1889

Thicknesse, P., *Observations on the Customs and
Manners of the French Nation*, 1766

Thrale, H. L., *The French Journals of Mrs Thrale and
Dr. Johnson*, edited by M. Tyson and H. Guppy,
Manchester University Press, 1932

Thrale, H. L., *Thraliana – The Diary of Mrs Hester Lynch
Thrale 1776–1809*, edited by K. C. Balderston,
Oxford University Press, 1944

Walpole, H., *The Letters of Horace Walpole*, edited by
P. Toynbee, 1905

Ward, J. W., *Letters of the Earl of Dudley to the Bishop
of Llandaff*, John Murray, 1841

Wilson, H., *Harriette Wilson's Memoirs of Herself and
Others*, Peter Davies, 1929

Wordsworth, D., *Journals of Dorothy Wordsworth*,
edited by W. Knight, Macmillan, 1897

Young, A., *Travels in France*, George Bell, 1890